CAMBRIDGE LIBRARY COLLECTION

Books of enduring scholarly value

History

The books reissued in this series include accounts of historical events and movements by eye-witnesses and contemporaries, as well as landmark studies that assembled significant source materials or developed new historiographical methods. The series includes work in social, political and military history on a wide range of periods and regions, giving modern scholars ready access to influential publications of the past.

A Descriptive Catalogue of the Manuscripts in the Library of Eton College

M. R. James (1862–1936) is probably best remembered as a writer of chilling ghost stories, but he was an outstanding scholar of medieval literature and palaeography, who served both as Provost of King's College, Cambridge, and as Director of the Fitzwilliam Museum, and many of his stories reflect his academic background. His detailed descriptive catalogues of manuscripts owned by colleges, cathedrals and museums are still of value to scholars today. This volume, first published in 1895, contains James' catalogue of the manuscript holdings of Eton College, where he himself was educated. No catalogue had been published since 1697, when 115 manuscripts were briefly noted; by James' time the collection had grown to 193. James provides information on the donors and the library building before going on to describe the manuscripts and their contents. His book is still sought after and this reissue will be welcomed by librarians and researchers alike.

Cambridge University Press has long been a pioneer in the reissuing of out-of-print titles from its own backlist, producing digital reprints of books that are still sought after by scholars and students but could not be reprinted economically using traditional technology. The Cambridge Library Collection extends this activity to a wider range of books which are still of importance to researchers and professionals, either for the source material they contain, or as landmarks in the history of their academic discipline.

Drawing from the world-renowned collections in the Cambridge University Library, and guided by the advice of experts in each subject area, Cambridge University Press is using state-of-the-art scanning machines in its own Printing House to capture the content of each book selected for inclusion. The files are processed to give a consistently clear, crisp image, and the books finished to the high quality standard for which the Press is recognised around the world. The latest print-on-demand technology ensures that the books will remain available indefinitely, and that orders for single or multiple copies can quickly be supplied.

The Cambridge Library Collection will bring back to life books of enduring scholarly value (including out-of-copyright works originally issued by other publishers) across a wide range of disciplines in the humanities and social sciences and in science and technology.

A Descriptive
Catalogue of the
Manuscripts in the
Library of Eton College

MONTAGUE RHODES JAMES

CAMBRIDGE
UNIVERSITY PRESS

CAMBRIDGE UNIVERSITY PRESS

Cambridge, New York, Melbourne, Madrid, Cape Town, Singapore,
São Paolo, Delhi, Dubai, Tokyo, Mexico City

Published in the United States of America by Cambridge University Press, New York

www.cambridge.org
Information on this title: www.cambridge.org/9781108027793

© in this compilation Cambridge University Press 2011

This edition first published 1895
This digitally printed version 2011

ISBN 978-1-108-02779-3 Paperback

A DESCRIPTIVE CATALOGUE

OF THE

MANUSCRIPTS

IN THE

LIBRARY OF ETON COLLEGE

𝔏onõon: C. J. CLAY AND SONS,
CAMBRIDGE UNIVERSITY PRESS WAREHOUSE,
AVE MARIA LANE.
𝔊lasgoõ: 263, ARGYLE STREET.

𝔏eipʒig: F. A. BROCKHAUS.
𝔑eõ 𝔜ork: MACMILLAN AND CO.

A

DESCRIPTIVE CATALOGUE

OF THE

MANUSCRIPTS

IN THE LIBRARY OF

ETON COLLEGE

BY

MONTAGUE RHODES JAMES, Litt.D.,

FELLOW OF KING'S COLLEGE, CAMBRIDGE; DIRECTOR OF THE FITZWILLIAM MUSEUM.

CAMBRIDGE:
AT THE UNIVERSITY PRESS.
1895

$\mathfrak{Cambridge}$:

PRINTED BY J. AND C. F. CLAY,

AT THE UNIVERSITY PRESS.

MEMORIAE

HENRICI SEXTI

PRINCIPIS SANCTI ET NOBILIS
MERITO HOC OPVSCVLVM DEDICO
ILLIVS ENIM MVNIFICENTIA
MIHI LICVIT NANCISCI
QVIDQVID AVT SCIENTIAE AVT AMICORVM
NACTVS FVERIM.

PREFACE.

THE important collection of Manuscripts described in this volume has never been catalogued at all in detail. In Bernard's *Catalogi Manuscriptorum Angliae et Hiberniae* (Oxford, 1697: Vol. II. p. 46) will be found the only attempt at a Catalogue which has yet seen the light. The name of the person who made the list is not given. There were then 115 MSS. in the Library, and the contents of these are briefly noted under 126 heads, some of the volumes being catalogued twice or three times over. The order followed is roughly alphabetical, beginning with Adelard and ending with Xenophon. I should be the last to criticise Bernard's list in an unfriendly spirit: his work is a very great one. For the history of English Libraries now dispersed—nay, even for the ascertaining of the contents of many which now exist, his volumes are indispensable: yet it is certain that the Catalogues which they contain are of very diverse merits; and it is undeniable that his Eton Catalogue is among those that are inadequate. For one thing, whereas in his time the College possessed 115 MSS., it now has 193.

Since 1697, as I said, no attempt at a systematic Catalogue has been made; but it should be mentioned that the Rev. F. St J. Thackeray's interesting papers on *Eton College Library* (reprinted from *Notes and Queries*) contain a survey of the manuscript classes.

It may seem curious that Uffenbach, who explored so many English Libraries in the last century, has told us nothing of the Eton books. He was not fortunate in his visit to Eton. He was unable to get a better idea of the name than 'Cato's College';

and was only introduced, it would seem, to the Boys' Library, which then consisted of little more than fifty volumes.

Of the history of the collection, and of the building in which it is housed, I might write at some length; but a very short summary of the facts must suffice.

First, as to the books. The sources from which they came, so far as I have been able to ascertain them, are seen in the *List of Donors and Owners*. William Horman and Sir Henry Wotton stand out pre-eminent as the two great benefactors of the Library. The latter has contributed nearly all the most valuable MSS. The bulk of his bequest consists of Greek and Italian MSS.: and many of these—perhaps all of them—were once the property of Bernardo Bembo, the father of Pietro Bembo. These Wotton no doubt bought at Venice. Two volumes are known to me which once formed part of the same collection, but did not come to Eton: one is a Horace at King's College (No. 34), the other, which I have never seen, is a Terence at Brasenose (No. 18), of the eleventh century—"bought," says Coxe's *Catalogue*, "of the heirs of Pietro Bembo at Venice in 1632," which date is probably wrong. The Horace was given by Wotton to Samuel Collins in 1630, and the Terence to William Hacwell.

Next, as to the building. The Founder's will provided for a Library in the East 'pane,' or walk of the Cloister: it was to be 52 feet long by 24 wide. This, however, was never built. The books belonging to the College were kept first in the vestry of the Chapel, then in "Election Hall" (where the painted glass appropriate to the different classes of books still remains in part); then in a room under Long Chamber: after that (in 1688, when David Loggan drew his view of the College) in the south-east part of the Cloister: and, lastly, they were transferred to the present building, which was constructed between 1725 and 1729, after the designs of one Mr Rowland.

In 1719 the chains were removed from the books "excepting the Founder's Manuscripts[1]."

---

[1] See, for the facts here summarized, Willis and Clark, *Architectural History of the University of Cambridge.*

Lastly, as to my own work. It has been a labour of love. The Eton Manuscripts were the first to which I had access. When I was an Eton boy, the College authorities generously allowed me to examine them. The kindness was a great one, and I hope it was not misplaced. The least I could have done in return was to put at their disposal such knowledge as they had helped me to gain; and this is what I have tried to do. That there are mistakes and omissions in this volume I have not the least doubt: yet I cannot but hope that there is also a good deal of information which will be helpful to scholars both in England and abroad.

My sincere thanks are due to the College for undertaking the printing of this Catalogue: and to the Provost, Dr Hornby, and the Vice-Provost and Librarian, Mr Warre-Cornish. The former has always been most kind in giving me access to the Library: while the latter has helped me and furthered my work in every possible way.

M. R. JAMES.

LIST OF DONORS, OWNERS, AND SCRIBES OF THE MSS.

Donors.		*No.*
William Aiscough, Bishop of Salisbury,	1438–50	28, 29
John Malberthorp, Fellow,	144...	47
William Wey, Fellow,	144...	76, ?99
Thomas Weston, Fellow,	1453	42
Peter Hopton,	1455	101
Richard Hopton, Fellow,	1477	39, 114
— Spenser,	1496	1, 2
Robert Elys,	1501	5
John Borowe, Fellow (?),	14...	120
Roger Lupton, Provost,	1540	131
William Horman, Fellow,	1535	24, 44, 48, 79, 80, 98, 119, 122, 126, 127, 148, ?171
Sir Henry Wotton, Provost,	1639	11, ?46, 85, 87, 88, 100, 110, 112, 113, 115, 118, ?121, 124, 128, 135–142, 146, 147, 149–159, 163, 165, 166, 172, 173, 174, 193
— Moyle,	1695	91
Thomas Horne, Fellow,	1713	21, 78
T. Richardson, Fellow,	1722	49–73, 90, 133
Edward Waddington, Bishop of Chichester, Fellow,	1731	111, 168
Henry Temple, Viscount Palmerston,	1750	22–95
Nicolas Mann,	1754	183, 186, 187
William Hetherington, Fellow,	1773	25
Edward Betham, Fellow,	1775–6	86, 143, 179
R. Huggett, Conduct and Librarian,	177...	144, ?183
George Henry Pitt,	1817	177
Anthony Storer,	182...	181
Lord Montague,	1833	188
E. C. Hawtrey,	1853	184

OWNERS.

1. *Monastic.*

Albans, St	25, 103
Belvoir (Lincolnshire)	48
Brescia, S. Apollonio	118
Chichester (?)	45
Farfa	124
Franciscans (Coventry)	108
,, (Lincolnshire)	170
,, (Sherborne)	33
Haverford	90
Merton Priory	123
Norwich (?)	45
Otteham (Praemonstr.)	43
Quarre	14
Reading (?)	84
Winchester College	91

2. *Private.*

Alcantieri, Claudio (?)	75
Ancona, Cyriacus of	141
Barett, Will.	80
Bathon., W. (*v.* Laud).	
Beaufort	114
Bembo, Bernardo	135, 137, ? 138, 147, ? 149, 151, 152, 153, 156
Bickerstaffe, Stuart	177
Bylton, Peter	39, 101
Canapede (?)	179
Carlisle, Frederick, Earl of,	181
Chicheley, T.	105
Cornario, Lud. Rig.	137
Cyriacus of Ancona	141
Delphini, Jo.	115, 124, 138
Edwardus de valle scolarium	32
Eliezur (?), J. Rogers	21
Ellys, Sir Richard	92–95
Flobern, Elizabeth	96
Gibbon, Henry	182
Hyle, Magister	27
John of Ragusa	144
Kempston, Nicholas	18, 36, 77, 117
Languscus, Jo.	137

Laud, William	90, 133
Linguscus, Jo.	137
Lysle, Sir John	24
Mareys, Tho.	105
Mauclerc, Dan.	144
,, Jac.	144
,, Joh. Hen.	144
Medici	157
Mocer (*or* Moyer), Joh.	105, 106
Nevelet, F. N.	144
Pabage, J.	91
,, W.	91
Parker, Matthew	123
Rogers (?), J.	21
Selby, R.	38
Seymour, Ed.	25
Sherard, Sir John	177
Smyth, Walter	74
Sugete, T.	17
Sukelyn, Jo.	127
Swan, Hen.	119
Sybbe, Will.	34
Sybley, J.	25
Sydeberne, J.	17
Thoresby, Hugo	90
Waller, Jo.	179
West	3
Wey, Will.	42
W. G.	102
Wouw, Barth. van	91

Scribes.

Agallianos	14...	141
Darellus		79
Doukas	1418?	144
Edyngtone, Rob.	1455	24
Forli, Valeriano di	1534	11, 100
Kempston, Nich.		18
Lorenzo di Stefano		136
Morton, Will.	1403	108
Sybbe, W.		34
Wodewarde		42

See also nos. 45, 92, 102, 149, 151, 161, 163, 165, 172, 182, 185

COMPARATIVE TABLES OF NUMBERING OF THE MSS.

I.

Present Number.	Cat. MSS. Angl.	Present Number.	Cat. MSS. Angl.	Present Number.	Cat. MSS. Angl.
	(ii. 46)	39	28 *b*?	105	16
1	31	40	*vac.*	106	19
2	31	41	79	107	18
3	89	42	43, 80	108	15 *sub fin.*
4	121	43	39, 60	109	110 *b*
5	7	44	3	110	113
6	?	45	41	111	*vac.*
7	20	46	8	112	44
8	71	47	22	113	73
9	91?	48	21	114	93
10	10	49–73	*vac.*	115	45
11	42	74	83	116	118
12	?	75	108	117	50
13	66	76	75	118	59
14	35	77	60?	119	65
15	110 *a*	78	*vac.*	120	14, 15, 24, 25, 29
16	109	79	102	121	37, 38
17	81	80	74	122	56
18	77	81	11	123	58
19	34	82	61	124	70
20	72	83	104	125	41
21	75	84	2	126	84
22	76	85	5	127	97
23	40	86	*vac.*	128	4
24	27	87	106	129	13
25	31 (?)	88	120	130	55
26	31	89	114	131	36
27	31	90	*vac.*	132	46
28	31	91	—	133	*vac.*
29	31	92–95	—	134	57
30	115	96	—	135	112
31	100	97	47	136	111
32	?	98	90	137	125
33	67	99	49, 124	138	87
34	69	100	88	139	78
35	117	101	17	140	107
36	98	102	62	141	116
37	68	103	64	142	126
38	28, 30	104	82	143	*vac.*

Present Number.	Cat. MSS. Angl.	Present Number.	Cat. MSS. Angl.	Present Number.	Cat. MSS. Angl.
144	—	161	1	178	—
145	9	162	vac.	179	—
146	51	163	123	180	—
147	12	164	vac.	181	—
148	vac.	165	96	182	6
149	119	166	53	183	vac.
150	101	167	vac.	184	—
151	94	168	—	185	48
152	85	169	32	186	vac.
153	86	170	92	187	—
154	105	171	63	188	—
155	52, 103	172	54	189	—
156	95	173	vac.	190	26
157	99	174	—	191	vac.
158	33	175	—	192	vac.
159	vac.	176	—	193	122
160	—	177	—		

II.

Cat. MSS. Angl.	Present Number.	Cat. MSS. Angl.	Present Number.	Cat. MSS. Angl.	Present Number.
1	161	26	190	51	146
2	84	27	24	52	155
3	44	28	38, 39?	53	166
4	128	29	120	54	172
5	85	30	38	55	130
6	182	31	1, 2, 25, 26, 27, 28, 29	56	122
7	5	32	169	57	134
8	46	33	158	58	123
9	145	34	19	59	118
10	10	35	14	60	43, 77
11	81	36	131	61	82
12	147	37	121	62	102
13	129	38	121	63	171
14	120	39	43	64	103
15	108, 120	40	23	65	119
16	105	41	45, 125	66	13
17	101	42	11	67	33
18	107	43	42	68	37
19	106	44	112	69	34
20	7	45	115	70	124
21	48	46	132	71	8
22	47	47	97	72	20
23	47	48	185	73	113
24	120	49	99	74	80
25	120	50	117	75	21, 76

Cat. MSS. Angl.	Present Number.	Cat. MSS. Angl.	Present Number.	Cat. MSS. Angl.	Present Number.
76	22	93	114	110	15, 109
77	18	94	151	111	136
78	139	95	156	112	135
79	41	96	165	113	110
80	42	97	127	114	89
81	17	98	36	115	30
82	104	99	157	116	141
83	74	100	31	117	35
84	126	101	150	118	116
85	152	102	79	119	149
86	153	103	155	120	88
87	138	104	83	121	4
88	100	105	154	122	193
89	3	106	87	123	163
90	98	107	140	124	99
91	9?	108	75	125	137
92	170	109	16	126	142

CORRIGENDA.

p. 3, l. 19,   *for* Apocr.   *read* Apoc.

,, ,, ,, 22,   ,, [C. M. A.] 10 ,,   89.

,, 19, lin. ult. ,,   ,,   vac. ,,   28, 30.

,, 20, l. 6,   ,, Sertonis   ,,   Serlonis.

,, 21, ,, 18,   ,, [C. M. A.] 80 ,,   43, 80.

,, ,, ,, 29,   ,,   ,,   60 ,,   39, 60.

,, 23, ,, 31,   ,,   ,,   22 ,,   22, 23.

,, 29, ,, 17,   ,,   ,,   12 ,,   2.

,, 30, ,, 17,   ,,   ,,   116 ,,   106.

,, 39, ,, 10,   ,,   ,,   124 ,,   49, 124.

,, 45, ,, 24,   ,,   ,,   120 ,,   110.

1, 2.   Bk. i. 1, 2.

BIBLIA SACRA.

Vellum, 16½ × 11½, ff. 176 and 160; double columns of 58 lines each. Cent. xiii. Vol. i. in 17 gatherings of 10 leaves and one of 6. Vol. ii. in 16 gatherings of 10 leaves.

Contents:

> Vol. i.   Interpretationes nominum (Ard—Zuzim), f. 1 gone, followed by four blank leaves.
> Jerome's Prologue, f. 10: Genesis to end of Ps. cl.
> Vol. ii.   Proverbs to Acts iii. 10 qui ad...

The Acts follow the Ep. to the Hebrews.

There are a few historiated initials, usually of good execution:

Vol. i.   1. *Prologue.* Initial, a nimbed man writing: on gold ground.

2. *Genesis.* Initial extending down the page, containing seven elliptical miniatures of the Days of Creation. In Nos. 1–4 Christ is holding the globe. In No. 5 he is standing, water on *R.* No. 6 Creation of Eve. No. 7 Christ seated.

In *Leviticus* the decorative initial retains its red silk guard.

Esdras I. is Ezra and Nehemiah in xviii. chapters.

Esdras II. is 1 Esdras of our Apocrypha, more commonly known now as 3 Esdras.

3. *Psalter. Beatus uir.* David playing the harp, gold ground. *Quid gloriaris* and *Dixit insipiens* both have decorative initials, as also *Domine exaudi* (ci.).

4. *Psalter. Dixit dominus.* Christ seated blessing: gold ground.

Vol. ii.   5. *Matthew.* Jesse asleep: from him springs a Tree with two figures in it, (1) of the Virgin, (2) of Christ seated blessing with book, beardless: gold ground.

The initials to 1 *Thess.* and 1 *Tim.* closely resemble each other: they contain dragons.

In Vol. i. f. 1*b* is the entry

Ex dono m*agistri* Spens*er* a° d*ni* 1496.

[C. M. A. 31.][1]

---

[1] These references in square brackets are to the *Catalogi Manuscriptorum Angliae et Hiberniae*, 1697.

3. Bk. 1. 3.

BIBLE HYSTORIAL.

Vellum, $17\frac{1}{8} \times 12\frac{1}{8}$, ff. 241, in double columns. Cent. xiv. (1380 ?).
Six leaves are lost, at the beginning of Cant. Ecclus. Matt. Phil.
and two in Micah. In gatherings of 12, 10, and 8 leaves.

This is the second volume of a Bible hystorial, in French:
being a translation of the *Historia Scholastica* of Peter Comestor
made by Guiart des Moulins in 1291–1295. This volume contains
the books from Proverbs ('Paraboles') to the Apocalypse.

The miniatures are of good average execution: their form is
that of a lozenge inscribed in a quatrefoil:

1. *Paraboles* (Proverbs). Four miniatures, together occupying half of f. 1 *a*.
   (*a*) Solomon and Rehoboam.
   (*b*) Solomon: before him three youths with a coffin. This is the first scene of a
well known mediaeval story (told in the *Gesta Romanorum*). The sons each claim their
father's property: the test imposed by Solomon is that each shall try to hit with an arrow
the heart (or right eye) of their father's corpse.
   (*c*) Two of the three sons about to shoot at their father's corpse, which hangs
on a tree: the youngest refuses (and so gains the inheritance).
   (*d*) The Biblical Judgment of Solomon.
2. *Ecclesiastes.* Solomon enthroned: a woman kneels to him.
   Cantiques: first leaf gone.
3. *Sapience.* A man kneels to receive a sword from a throned figure.
   Ecclesiasticus: first leaf gone.
4. *Ysaie.* The prophet seated cross-legged and bound: two men are sawing his head
with a frame-saw.
5. *Jeremie.* Jeremiah as a youth watching sheep: Christ appears to him above.
6. *Lamentations.* Jeremiah points to the gates of Jerusalem: other figures behind
him.
7. *Baruch.* Addresses six men: he is represented as old.
8. *Ezekiel.* The prophet looks at the vision of the four cherubim who hold scrolls
with the names of the Evangelists.
9. *Daniel.* He is pointing Nebuchadnezzar upward to Christ in the sky. This picture has a good diapered ground.
   Osee: no miniature.
10. *Joel.* Watching sheep: Christ's head appears in the sky.
11. *Amos.* In bed: Christ's head seen above, covered with blood.
    Obadiah, Jonah, Micah: the miniatures are gone.
12. *Nahum.* Walking in a river: three men watch him.
13. *Habakkuk.* The prophet caught up by the angel (see *Bel and the Dragon*): he
holds a vessel in each hand. This scene is usually called the Rapture of Habakkuk.

14. *Zephaniah.* Writing at a desk.
15. *Haggai.* Holds a scroll with *Ave Maria* upon it.
16. *Zechariah.* Holds a blank scroll.
17. *Malachi.* At a desk, reading the ten commandments.
18. 1 *Macc.* A kneeling man beheaded : probably refers to 1 Macc. ii. 24.
    2 *Macc.:* no miniature.
    S. Matthew: first leaf gone.
19. *S. Mark.* Writing: the lion by him.
20. *S. Luke.* A similar picture: the ox by him.
21. *S. John.*   ,,   ,,   : the eagle by him.
22. *Romans.* S. Paul preaching to a crowd.
23. 1 *Cor.* S. Paul enters a city (Corinth).
24. 1 *Tim.* S. Paul before an Emperor (Nero).
25. *Gal* S. Paul preaching.
26. *Eph.* S. Paul arriving at a city (Ephesus).
The other Epistles have no pictures.
27. *Acts.* S. Luke directs the attention of Theophilus (a crowned man) to Christ
ascending.
28. *Apocr.* The beast with seven heads and ten horns.
The work degenerates towards the end of the volume.
As a fly-leaf at the end is the motto *Une sans Plus* (cent. xvi.).

[C. M. A. 10.]

4. Bk. 1. 4.

A DICTIONARY, ETC.

Vellum, $10\frac{1}{2} \times 7\frac{1}{4}$, ff. 126. Cent. xv.

1. An Index, beginning with the word *celare* and ending with
vespertilio, f. 1: in 3 columns to a page.

It is in 12 leaves a⁸ (wants 1–3) b⁸ (wants 8).

2. Variae uerborum significaciones, f. 13.

A dictionary, imperfect in the middle and at the end, in double
columns, from *Abba* to *Vath*, in quires of 12 leaves.

3. A work on Scripture History from the Creation, f. 86.

In several books: imperfect. In double columns: quires of 8
leaves.

At the beginning on f. 86*a* is 'pater et filius et spiritus sanctus'
also the name 'west.'

The prologue begins: In precedentib*us* p*re*missa desc*ri*pcio*ne*
originis et dest*ru*ccionis artium et q*uoru*nd*a*m alioru*m* ortu*m* et
occasu*m* omn*i*u*m* regnoru*m*.

Lib. i. begins: Primus liber tractat de misteriis rerum gestarum ab inicio usque ad abraham, continens capitula 19.

It wants from Lib. viii. 2 to Lib. xii. 1 and the end of Lib. xiii.

Expl. et si uenerit in 2ª uigilia et si in 3ª uenerit et ita inuenerit, beatus ergo seruus ille: uigilias uocat ad....

[C. M. A. 121.]

5. Bk. 1. 5.

S. AMBROSIUS SUPER *Beati Immaculati* (Ps. cxviii. *Lat.* cxix. *Heb.*).

Vellum, 13½ × 9¼, ff. 167, double columns.   Cent. xi.   In quires of 8 leaves (i–xviii numbered *prima manu*).   Binding, boards and stamped leather with medallion of crowned heads, lettered HERCVLIS and VENA (?).   This binding, which must be of cent. xvi., occurs on many of the MSS.: it will be referred to henceforth as H.V.

The flyleaves are from a MS. concordance to the Vulgate (cent. xv.) which is often used in connexion with the H.V. binding.

An initial L at the beginning of the text seems rather Celtic in character.   The hand is narrow and rather pointed at first; towards the end of the volume it becomes rounder, thicker, and more sloping.

On f. 1*a* is:

Liber collegii de Eton de dono magistri Roberti Elys aº dⁱ 1501.

[C. M. A. 7.]

6. Bk. 1. 6.

S. AUGUSTINUS IN PSALMOS 1–50.

Vellum, 16⅞ × 11½, ff. 154, double columns.   Cent. xv. (?).   The hand seems English, rubricated initials.   Binding H.V.   In quires of 8 leaves.   On the fly-leaf: ...Aug in psalmos et incipit in 2º fo. *Quam montem.*   At the end a note of the price:

xiˢ xiᵈ pa*r*ue (?) tre (? parmentrie) et...pro ligatura xxxiiijᵈ.

[C. M. A. ?]

7. Bk. 1· 7·

S. AUGUSTINUS IN PSALMOS 51—100.

Vellum, $16\frac{1}{8} \times 11\frac{1}{8}$, ff. 191, double columns. Cent. xiii. The hand is English. There are decorative initials, chiefly in blue; some have been cut out. The fly-leaves are from the Concordance, and from a large Gospel-book. In 24 quires of 8 leaves, numbered in Roman figures: xv. is of 7 leaves.

[C. M. A. 20.]

8. Bk. 1. 8.

ROB. GROSTHED (GROSSETETE) IN C. PSALMOS.

Vellum, 15 × 10, ff. 217, double columns. Cent. xv. Decorative initials: that of f. 1*a* has on a patterned ground these letters in gold *t. ihc. b.* Binding H.V.

An Index begins on f. 206.

[C. M. A. 71.]

9. Bk. 1. 9.

COMMENTARIUS IN LIBRUM PSALMORUM.

Vellum, $13\frac{1}{4} \times 9\frac{3}{4}$, ff. 183. Cent. xiii–xiv. In quires of 8 leaves. Text surrounded by commentary: rubricated and flourished initials, that to Ps. cix. (cx.) *Dixit Dominus* has three rude heads symbolising the Trinity. The Commentary is, I think, the *glossa ordinaria*. *Inc.* Cum omnes prophetas sancti spiritus reuelatione constet esse locutos. *Expl.* Vite eterne uox est omnis spiritus laudet dominum. Amen. hic ex.

[C. M. A. 91 (?).]

10. Bk. 1. 10.

R. HAMPOLE ON THE PSALMS.

See *post*.

[C. M. A. 10.]

11. Bk. I. II.

DEMETRII CYDONII ORATIO DE CONTEMNENDA MORTE.

Paper, 12½ × 8¾, ff. 18, 35 pp. written. Cent. xvi. (1539).

τοῦ σοφωτάτου καὶ λογιωτάτου κυρίου Δημητρίου τοῦ κυδονίου
λόγος ὅπως ἄλογον τὸ τοῦ θανάτου δέος ἀποδεικνύων.

Colophon: ἀδελφὸς βαλεριανὸς φορολιβιεὺς ὁ ἀλβινοῦ ἔγραψε ἐν
μοναστηρίῳ τοῦ ἁγίου ἀντωνίου ἐνετίω(ν) ἔτη ‚αφλθ (1539). On this
scribe see further on Bl. I. 19. The author died after 1384.

The oration was first printed with the *Irrisio* of Hermias by
Raphael Seiler at Basel in 1553. See Fabricius, *Bibl. Gr.* ed.
Harles, xi. 401.

[C. M. A. 42.]

12. Bk. I. 12.

S. GREGORII MAGNI MORALIUM LIBB. xvii–xxxiii. 17.

Vellum, 14 × 10, ff. 232, double columns. Cent. xiii. (early).
The hand is English: in xxix. quires of 8 leaves, numbered i–xxix.
Fly-leaves from a law-book of cent. xiv. in Italian hand.

Ends: ne forte in initio murmurationis excedat memoretur que
timeat (xxxiii. 17).

There are splendid initials at the beginning of each book: see
especially books xxviii–xxx. At book xviii. is a good picture in
the initial of Christ seated blessing, on gold ground, with cross-
nimbus.

[C. M. A. ?]

13. Bk. I. 13.

S. GREGORII MAGNI MORALIA.

Vellum, 16 × 11, ff. 213, double columns. Cent. xiv.

Contents:

Capitula	f. 1
Visio Taionis	8
Moralia	9

Collation: a⁸ i¹²–xvi¹² xvii¹²⁺¹. Fly-leaves from the Concordance: very good flourished initials of red and blue. At the end:
Laus tibi sit Christe quoniam liber explicit iste.

[C. M. A. 66.]

14. Bk. 2. 1.

CANTOR IN GENESIM, EXODUM ET LEVITICUM.

Vellum, 15 × 10⅜, ff. 200, double columns. Cent. xiii. Blank fly-leaves. In the binding a leaf of a law MS. In quires of 8 leaves, numbered i–xxv., *prima manu*. The last leaves have suffered much from damp. At the end on a fly-leaf are some hexameters enumerating the books of the Bible. At the beginning is :

> Est de Quadraria *liber iste crucisque* (erased) Maria.
> Sit reus an*te* de*u*m qui ti*bi* tollat eum.

This shews that the volume belonged to Quarre (or Quarrer) Abbey in the Isle of Wight (Cistercian) founded in 1132.

[C. M. A. 35.]

15. Bk. 2. 2.

RADULPHUS FLAVIACENSIS IN LEVITICUM : LIBRI xx.

Vellum, 13¾ × 10, ff. 250, double columns. Cent. xii. (late). Binding of cent. xv., brown leather on wooden boards. The hand seems English : in quires of 10 leaves (?). Good decorative initials, e.g. on f. 3 *b* : one at the beginning has been cut out.

On the verso of the last leaf is : primus p*artus* (sic) 2° gradu et in sinistro.

[C. M. A. 110.]

16. Bk. 2. 3.

RABANUS IN NUMEROS, DEUTERONOMIUM, JOSUE, JUDICES, RUTH, REGES, THOBIAM, JUDITH, HESTER.
CANTOR IN ESDRAM, NEEMIAM, PARALIPOMENA.
RABANUS IN MACCABAEOS.

Vellum, 14 × 10½, ff. 200, double columns. Cent. xii. In quires of 8 leaves : the first gone, the rest numbered ii–xxvi. *prima manu*. Ends in 2 Macc. iii. occidentales. Has suffered much from damp. Binding of cent. xv. Fly-leaves from a law MS.

[C. M. A. 109.]

17. Bk. 2. 4.

HUGO CARDINALIS DE VYENNA SUPER LIBROS SALOMONIS.

Vellum, 12⅜ × 9, ff. 323 and 1, in double columns. Cent. xiv. in two hands, the second beginning at f. 92. In quires of 8 leaves. Binding H.V. Fly-leaves from Concordance.

On the recto of the last leaf in the lower corner is written :

deo gratias legi totum aº 1493 18 die junii claudo.

and : Iste est Johannes Sydeberne et sic dixit Tomas Sugete.

[C. M. A. 81.]

18. Bk. 2. 5.

HOLCOT IN LIBRUM SAPIENTIAE.

Vellum, 14⅛ × 9⅛, ff. 224, double columns. Cent. xv. Rubricated initials. Binding H.V.

In the beginning :

liber quondam magistri Nicholai Kempston aº dⁿⁱ 1477 nunquam vendendus secundum ultimam voluntatem defuncti sed gratis et libere occupandus a sacerdotibus instructis in lege domini ad predicandum verbum dei successive ab vno sacerdote ad alterum sacerdotem absque omni precio quamdiu duraverit.

Orate pro anima eius.

The same inscription is quoted from MS. Jes. Coll. Oxon. 116 by Hardy *Catalogue of Materials* ii., lxiv. See also MS. Rawlinson A. 446 and S. John's Coll. Camb. MS. A. 15 : also below.

Contents :

1. Index with additions by Kempston.
2. Text of Holcot.
3. An addition in the same hand, ff. 213–214a.
4. Index rerum, at the end of which is :

   Explicit tabula lecture Holcoti super librum sapiencie scripta per mag. Nicholaum Kempston anno domini millesimo quadringentesimo septuagesimo quinto.

5. Another ill-written index on 4½ leaves.

   Explicit tabula fratris Rob. Holcoti super librum sapiencie de ordine fratrum predicatorum doctoris sacre theologie conventus norhamtonie.

In the binding at the end is written a record of an obit for A. Marshall, Vicar of All Saints, Worcester.   Bishop Philip Morgan's name is mentioned.

[C. M. A. 77.]

19.   Bk. 2. 6.

CANTOR IN ISAIAM, JEREMIAM, DANIELEM, XII PROPHETAS.

Vellum, $14\frac{1}{4} \times 10\frac{1}{8}$, ff. 280, double columns.   Cent. xii.   Binding H.V.   Fly-leaves from Concordance, and two from a xiith century MS. in double columns: *Omelia in Genesim* ii. concerning the ark.

Contents :

1. Cantor in Is., Jer., Dan., Hos.—Mal. in two or three hands : has suffered from damp.
2. A Tract on the Book of Wisdom.   Inc. Quecunque scripta.

An old table of contents enumerates besides the following tracts, now lost :

Summa Joh. Wallensis ad omne genus hominum.
Albertanus de arte dicendi et tacendi.
Melybeus et prudentia de consolatione et consilio (cp. Chaucer's *Persones Tale*).
Imago mundi.
Parisiensis de prebendis.
De pluralitate beneficiorum.
De conuersione peccatoris ad deum.

On a fly-leaf in large xvth cent. letters :

Cantor in Esaiam et Jeremiam.

[C. M. A. 34.]

20.   Bk. 2. 7.

HAYMO IN ESAIAM.

Vellum, $13 \times 9\frac{1}{2}$, ff. 176, double columns.   Cent. xii., in an ugly hand.   Flourished initials, many in light blue.   Binding like that of No. 21.   In quires of 8 leaves.   Fly-leaves from a law MS.

Contents :

1. Haymo in Esaiam . . . . f. 1
2. Alexandri prioris de Essebie (Easby in Yorkshire) liber festiualis .   166
    Inc.   Omnia cum nequeam sanctorum scribere gesta
           Pauca breui calamo scribere nitar ego.

The tract is in elegiacs, with prologues in prose and verse.

The feasts described begin with S. Andrew and end with S. Katherine and the *Transitio* to the second book. Ends *Expl.* liber primus.

3. Notes (*a*) on the attitude of the fingers in blessing, (*b*) on the words Triclinium, Lenticula, etc.

[C. M. A. 72.]

21.   Bk. 2. 8.

S. HIERONYMUS IN DANIELEM, ETC.

Vellum, 15 × 11, ff. 338, double columns.   Cent. xi–xii.   In quires of 20 leaves (two lost).

Contents :

1. Hieronymus in Danielem et xii. prophetas.   One leaf of the prologue is lost, and after f. 47 is a note : desiderantur folia quaedam abrupta interpretatione a fine cap. 1 (osee) usque ad vers. 15 cap. 4.

2. Ambrosius de obseruantia episcoporum *siue* Pastorale Ambrosii : in another hand.

3. Questio s. Ieronimi de induratione cordis Pharaonis et de aliis iiii. questionibus.

4. (fol. ult.) Ieronimus in annalibus ebreorum de xv. signis xv. dierum precedentium diem iudicii.

5. (A prophecy).   P·P·P·S·S·S·V·V·V·V·V·V·V·F·F·F·R·R·R·R·[R·]. Pars · patrie · profecta est · salus · secum · sullata est · veniet · victor · validus · vincet · vires · vestre · vrbis · ferro · fame · frigore · regale · regnum · Romanorum · ruit · Roma.

On f. 1 : Sum liber Johannis Rogers (erased) Eliezur 1594.   On first fly-leaf : 1713. Dedit Collegio B. M. de Etona Tho. Horne Soc.

[C. M. A. 75.]

22.   Bk. 2. 9.

S. HIERONYMUS IN XII. PROPHETAS.

Vellum, 15¼ × 10½, ff. 216 (209 + 7 blank), double columns. Cent. xiv.   In quires of 12 leaves, numbered as Bk. 1. 12.   On the fly-leaves are many pencil notes of cent. xiv., xv.   On f. 1 a xvth cent. note.   Liber Jeronimi super xii. prophetas etc. incipit in 2do folio *tue prudencie*.   At the bottom of f. 1 of the text :

L. Jeronimus super xij prophetas   H (erased).

[C. M. A. 76.]

23. Bk. 2. 10.

XII. PROPHETAE CUM GLOSSA.

Vellum, 14 × 9¼, ff. 114 (110 + 4 blank), text and two sets of notes. Cent. xiii–xiv. In quires of 8, 6 and 4 leaves. Erased monastic mark on the fly-leaf, also a distich on the names of the prophets :

Ose · Joel · Amos · Abdi · Jon · atque Micheas ·
Naum · Abacuk · Sophoni · Agge · Zachar · Malachias.

[C. M. A. 40.]

24. Bk. 2. 11.

BERENGAUDUS SUPER APOCALYPSIM, ETC.

Vellum, 14½ × 9¼, ff. 236 : double columns. Cent. xv. (1455). In quires of 12 (a–t) and one (v) of 8.

Contents :

1. "Belingarius" in Apocalypsim, in Latin and English . . f. 1
2. Sermones Odonis de tempore et sanctis 79
With index of the sermons and a later index rerum.

Colophon : Expliciunt sermones Odonis de Cancia quondam Archiepiscopi Cantuariensis scripte per Dominum Robertum Edyngtone infra hospicium strenui militis Johannis Lysle apud Wodehouse iuxta Arden in vigilia S^{ti} Laurencii martiris per ipsum dominum Robertum finaliter conscripte anno domini millesimo cccc^{mo} quinquagesimo quinto hā Ame*n* ·є·

On f. 1. Liber Willelmi Horman.

[C. M. A. 27.]

25. Bk. 3. 1.

BIBLIA SACRA.

Vellum, 13 × 9¼, ff. 498, in double columns, in two hands. Cent. xiii.

The vellum and writing are Italian : the miniatures French.

The volume was presented by William Hetherington in 1773. The text is preceded by the 'Doctrina ad cognitionem correctionis biblie' and followed by the 'Interpretationes nominum' f. 458.

The order of the groups of books in the New Testament is Evv., Paul, Acts, Cath., Apoc.

The illustrated initials are an interesting series: they run as follows:

1. *Prol.* A monk writing.
2. *Gen.* Containing 8 quatrefoils with gold grounds: (*a*) Christ holding two globes, light and dark; (*b*) holding a globe with land and water shown; (*c*) creating trees; (*d*) sun and moon; (*e*) birds; (*f*) Eve, and also beasts; (*g*) blessing: (*h*) the Crucifixion. Down each side of the initial are seven half-quatrefoils with half-lengths of prophets.
3. *Exod.* L. Amram, C. Moses in the ark, on water, R. Jochebed.
4. *Lev.* L. a man in a doorway, R. Moses, horned.
5. *Num.* A man speaks to Moses.
6. *Deut.* Moses, horned, reads the Law to the people.
7. *Jos.* Above, a nimbed figure (Christ) speaks to an attendant (Joshua): below, a man in bed (the body of Moses).
8. *Jud.* Warriors, and a prophet (?).
9. *Ruth.* Elimelech and Naomi and the sons set off to Moab.
10. *1 Sam.* Hannah praying, R. Eli at altar.
11. *2 Sam.* David orders the Amalekite to be slain.
12. *1 K.* David in bed: two figures (Abishag and a courtier) stand over him.
13. *2 K.* Ahaziah in bed, sending two men.
14. *1 Chr.* A crowd of figures. *2 Chr.* Decorative.
15. *Ezra.* A building scene.
16. *Neh.* Nehemiah as cupbearer before Artaxerxes.
17. *Tob.* Tobit blinded by the swallows.
18. *Judith.* Beheads Holofernes.
19. *Esther.* Touches the sceptre of Ahasuerus.
20. *Job.* Seated on the dunghill addresses his friends.
21. *Psalms.* David plays the harp.
22. *Prov.* Solomon chastises Rehoboam.
23. *Eccl.* Solomon throned, two attendants.
24. *Cant.* A boy addresses a woman.
25. *Wisd.* Solomon addresses a man with sword.
26. *Ecclus.* A man seated, with cup.
27. *Isa.* Sawn asunder by two men: he is bound to a pillar.
28. *Jer.* Christ touches his mouth.
29. *Lam.* Jeremiah seated at the gate of Jerusalem.
30. *Ezek.* In bed: five men before him: above, two censers, a wheel and a hand.
31. *Dan.* In the den.
32. *Hosea.* Embraces Gomer.
33. *1 Macc.* Mattathias dying speaks to his sons.
34. *Matt.* Jesse in bed: the tree springs from him containing four half-figures in

ellipses, on gold ground. The lowest is the Virgin, crowned: two are kings: the fourth is a prophet (?) in a cap: a very fine initial.

35. *Mark.* The Baptism: S. Mark, a lion below him.
36. *Luke.* Zacharias and the angel.
37. *John.* Christ seated: below, John: below him, the Eagle.
38. *Rom.* Paul with sword.
39. *2 Cor.* ,, ,,
40. *Heb.* Paul addresses a crowd of Jews on *L.*
41. *Acts.* The Apostles in a group.
42. *James and Jude.* Figures with books.
43. *Rev.* John sits writing: seven towers (or candlesticks) behind.

26. Bk. 3. 2.

BIBLIA SACRA.

Vellum, 13⅜ × 9, ff. 362, 3 columns: decorative initials. Cent. xii–xiii. In quires of 10 and 8 leaves.

This is by far the finest Vulgate in the collection. The writing and ornaments are very fine, and the contents and aspect of the book remarkable.

The number of 'versus' in each book is stated at the end, and the rest of the leaf left blank.

The order of the books is as follows:

Prologue.
Genesis to ii Paralipomenon.
Isaiah.
Jeremiah.
Baruch. Incipit liber baruch notarii Ieremie prophete. De oratione et sacrificio pro vita nabuchodonosor.
Epistle of Jeremiah.
Lamentations: prefixed to which is an explanation of the Hebrew alphabet.
Ezekiel.
Daniel: divided into 'visiones'; and with the apocryphal additions obelized.
The twelve prophets.
Job.
Ezra, Nehemiah, both called 'primus esdre.'
Esther (with additions obelized).
2 Esdras (= 1 Esdras).
A blank leaf is cut away here.
Proverbs. Eccl. Cant. Wisdom. Ecclus.
Oratio Salomonis ('Et inclinavit' . . 1 Kings viii.).
Tobit. Judith. 1, 2 Maccabees.
Preliminary matter to the Psalter, occupying 15 leaves.

The Psalter in three versions.   Gal., Rom., Hebr., with Ps. cli. in all three.
Cantica: ezechie, anne, moysi, abachuc, moysi (Deut. xxxiii.).
The beginnings of the Epistles and Gospels for the year.
Jerome's Letter to Damascus, and memorial verses on the Eusebian Canons.
The Eusebian Canons, called here 'Diatessaron,' in gold frames.
Evv.   Act.   Cath. Epp.   Apoc.
Prologues to Romans, and 26 verses by Damasus on S. Paul.
Paul. Epp.   Hebr.   Epistle to the Laodiceans.

On fol. 1, in red:

'hunc codicem dedit domn*us* mathias p*r*ior sa*n*cto albano q*u*em q*u*i ei abstulerit aut titulu*m* deleue*r*it anathema sit.   am*en*.'

In the xvth or xvith century it belonged to Johannes Sybley. On verso of fly-leaf, under the book-plate is: Edwarde Seymour, 27 August 1582.

There are a good many marginal notes.

[C. M. A. 31.]

27.   Bk. 3. 3.

BIBLIA SACRA.

Vellum, 12¾ × 8¾, ff. 388: double columns.   Cent. xii.   Fly-leaves from a law MS.   At f. 370*b* begin the *Interpretationes nominum*, and *Capitula*.

All the prologues are at the beginning of the volume.   The order of books in the O.T. is Gen.—Esther, Tob., Jud., Macc., Isa.—Mal. Job, Parab.—Ecclus. Oratio Salomonis, Psalmi.

The only figured initials are:

1. *Prol.* A Bishop with mitre and crosier seated : gold ground.
2.   ,,   A man and monkey.
3. *Genesis.* The seven days of creation: gold grounds: in Nos. 1–5 Christ is holding the globe.

On a fly-leaf: Liber mag. hyle vicarii collegii S^{ti} Georgii infra castrum de Windesor super quo ego Jo. Esterfeld canonicus ibidem exposui domino Jho...(?) petyt capellano s. x.s de pecunia m*a*gistri stoke.

[C. M. A. 31.]

28, 29. Bk. 3. 4, 5.

BIBLIA SACRA.

Vellum (uterine), $10\frac{5}{8} \times 7\frac{1}{4}$, two volumes, ff. 519, and ff. 520, in quires of 16 leaves, text and comment. Cent. xiii–xiv.

Vol. 1. Genesis—Ps. cl.
A figured initial in Genesis, representing the seven days of creation.
Five leaves in Exodus mutilated.

Vol. 2. Esaias—ii. Maccabaeorum.

On the fly-leaf: Liber Coll. Regal. beate Marie de Etona iuxta Wyndesor ex dono Willelmi episcopi Sarum. This is Will. Aiscough (1438–1450).

[C. M. A. 31.]

30. Bk. 3. 6.

SEPTUPLUM.

Vellum, $14 \times 9\frac{1}{2}$, ff. 105 in quires of 8: text in 2 columns surrounded by comment. Cent. xv. English hand.

Inc. Subuectiuam tabulam fragilitatis humane in mundi pelago carnis absortus uorticibus. It is a tract on the seven deadly sins. Binding, the original white skin on boards, has had a label on the last cover: chain-mark at lower *R.* corner of first cover.

There is a MS. of this work, dated 1412, at Univ. Coll. Oxford (no. lxxi).

[C. M. A. 115.]

31. Bk. 3. 7.

NAPIER ON THE APOCALYPSE, IN ITALIAN.

Paper, $13\frac{1}{2} \times 8$, ff. 140. Cent. xvii. It is a Commentary on the Apocalypse by John Napier of Merchiston (rendered as Nonpareil or Nonsuch), dedicated to James VI. of Scotland. It was translated into French by George Thomson and into Italian by P. M. V.

Contents:

The Commentary	f. 1
Index	f. 92
Quattro Armonie (on the Apocalypse again).	

[C. M. A. 100.]

32. Bk. 3. 8.

S. Bernardi etc. Tractatus.

Vellum, $11\frac{1}{4} \times 7\frac{3}{4}$, ff. 94 + 120 (two volumes in one).   Cent. xiii. and cent. xiv–xv.   Fly-leaves from two late MSS.

Part I. in quires of 12 leaves: in several hands of an Italian look.

1.	S. Bernardi Quo studio et affectu orandus sit deus . . . f.	1
2.	meditaciones	3
3.	meditacio de redempcione humana . . .	9
4.	notabilitates moralium beati Gregorii	11
5.	meditacio Bernardi de diligendo deo	19
6.	xviii libri de uitis patrum sub compendio	22
7.	meditacio ad concitandum timorem	38
8.	deploracio amisse uirginitatis	39
9.	meditacio Bernardi de planctu B. V. M.	42
10.	de diciplina monachorum siue apologeticon	45
11.	Anselmus de similitudinibus	48
12.	Anselmi cur deus homo: in two hands	50
13.	prefacio exhortationum Bernardi ad Eugenium (= Bernardus de consideratione)	71

At the top of f. 1*a* is: Edwardus de valle scolarium ordine fecit quod sumam s... et incipit 'letabor ego super eloquia' et thema est Sicut letancium omnium habitacio.

Part. II.   Wallensis super Psalmos, in quires of 12, 10 and 16 leaves.

Prol. inc.   Beatus qui custodit uerba prophetie libri huius.

On a fly-leaf at the beginning of the whole volume: iii. id. octobris anno domini m°·cc°·lx°·i° fui admissus cum custode. Anno domini m·cc·lxv. fui institutus.... The tops of the letters are cut off. Also there are two charms (1) for toothache "a. p. petrus supra petram sedebat" etc., (2) for bleeding at the nose: on the words bironis and bironixa, and a prayer in French (five lines) Duce dame saÿnt marie virgine.

[C. M. A.?]

33. Bk. 3. 9.

S. GREGORII DIALOGI, ETC.

Vellum, $10\frac{3}{4} \times 6\frac{1}{2}$, ff. 159 (quires of 8): cent. xii., xiii. The hand is English. Binding H.V.

Contents:

1. Gregorii Dialogi de Miraculis iv. . . . . . . f. 1
2. Hieronymi actus captiui monachi 98
3. Anon. de S. Frontonio . . . . 101 *b*
4. Hieronymi vita Pauli primi heremitae . . . . . 103 *b*
5. Vita B. Antonii ex graeco Athanasii 108
6. Hieronymi Vita S. Hilarionis . . . . 147 *b*

On the last leaf is written a Letter of Fraternity of 1256. Omnibus Christi fidelibus has literas uisuris uel audituris m. humilis prior Syreburnensis et eiusdem loci conuentus eternam in domino salutem. Nouerit uniuersitas uestra quod nos caritatis intuitu recepisse in fratres et sorores nostros hugonem de bellomonte burg. Vinton. et archebaud. cum vxoribus suis Alicia scilicet et Matilda. Concedentes eisdem plenariam participationem omnium bonorum spiritualium etc. (17 lines). Datum a. d. m°. cc°. l°. vi°.

[C. M. A. 67.]

34. Bk. 3. 10.

S. GREGORII HOMILIAE, ETC.

Vellum, $11\frac{1}{2} \times 8\frac{5}{8}$, ff. 199 (103 + 96): cent. xv. Two volumes bound in one. Binding, stamped leather with hatched lines.

1. S. Gregorii Homiliae in Ezechielem 22: in double columns: quires of 8, 10, and 14 leaves: ff. 103: signature d wants the sixth leaf (blank).

2. Fasciculus Morum per Will. Sybbe de parochia de Wisbich, scriptus 1443: ff. 96: single lines, quires of 8 leaves. It is dedicated to a "Frater" and divided into seven 'particulae.' At the end, on f. 88, is "Finis sermonum est hec colleccio morum : hic explicit liber qui vocatur Fasciculus morum scriptus per Willm Sybbe capellanum parochie de Wysebech : cuius anime Jhesus filius uirginis marie propicietur et perducat ad gaudia eterne vite. Anno domini millesimo cccc^{mo} quadragesimo tercio."

This colophon is followed by a long sermon interspersed, like all the rest of the work, with *narraciones*. English renderings of Latin phrases often occur. A quire is wanting at the end. At the beginning is 'assit principio sancta maria meo.'

[C. M. A. 69.]

35.   Bk. 3. 11.

S. Thomae quaedam.

Vellum, 12¾ × 9½, ff. 178 in double columns : quires of 8 and 12 leaves. Cent. xv. and xiv. (?). Fly-leaves from a large folio of xiith or xiiith century : an inscription shewing the provenance is erased.

 1. S. Thomas Aquin. de spiritualibus creaturis. Cent. xv.
 2. „ „ de potentia dei.
 3. „ „ de malo (imperfect : ends in lib. xiv.).
 4. (f. 167) Expositio Egidii. *Inc.* sicut philosophus dicit in x. ethicorum (ff. 12). Cent. xiv. ?

At end : explicit liber causarum. Amen.

[C. M. A. 117.]

36.   Bk. 3. 12.

Tabula Martini, etc.

Vellum, 11¾ × 8, ff. 135 and 103 in double columns. Cent. xiv., xv.

 1. Tabula Fratris Martini super decreta et decretales. Possibly in an Italian hand : ff. 135, in quires mostly of 12 leaves.
 2. Questiones Sancti Thome :
  i. de Malo.
  ii. de spiritualibus creaturis.
 ff. 103 in quires of 12, 6 and 10 leaves.
 The volume belonged to Kempston, and has his inscription, as in Bk. 2. 5.

[C. M. A. 98.]

37. Bk. 4. 1.

S. Gregorii Dialogi, etc.

Vellum, $10\frac{3}{8} \times 7\frac{1}{8}$, ff. 130 (quires of 8 and one of 2 leaves): single lines, 27 to a page. Cent. xii. Fly-leaves from a glossary of the Old Testament of cent. xiii. Binding as Bk. 3. 10.

S. Gregorii Magni Dialogorum Libri iv.	f. 1
S. Augustini liber decem chordarum	116 b

[C. M. A. 68.]

38. Bk. 4. 2.

S. Bernardi Homiliae, etc.

Vellum, $11\frac{1}{8} \times 7\frac{3}{4}$, ff. 214, double columns: quires of 8 leaves, numbered i–xxvii. Cent. xii. On the verso of the last leaf are entries of pledges and prices, thus:

Cum tribus C^{ts} 2° fo. primi *exire*: 2° fo. 2^{di} *dissidenciam*: 2° 6ta fo. 3^{tii} *de me det*. xxvj^s viij^d precium x^s.

Caucio domini Roberti Selby exposita in cista exo*ni*e Anno domini m° cccc° lx°·xx° v° die mensis octobris et habet 3ta 6ta 2° primi *exire* 2° fo 2^i *dissidenciam* 2° fol 3^i *de me det*. Emptus pro xxvj^s viij^d.

This volume was, then, pledged by Selby along with three others, of which the opening words of the second leaf in each case are here given.

S. Bernardi Homiliae lxxxii.	f. 1
Prefatio mag. Roberti Pull (? Pulleyn) de obsidione sirie . .	136 b
Two more sermons by the same	139
Magistri Hugonis homiliae iv. Tempus flendi etc.	151 b
Libellus B. Augustini de iv uirtutibus karitatis	152
Liber B. Pape Leonis de conflictu uitiorum atque uirtutum . .	154 b
Sermo mag. Robert Pull(eyn). Quatuor reges	162
Eiusdem sermo	164 b
Tractatus mag. Hugonis Parisiacensis super Lamentationes Jeremie, non tamen continue	168
Twelve homilies or extracts of varying length without author's name. One is 'de pallio Helie'	204

The hand is very good, probably French.

[C. M. A. *vac.*]

39. Bk. 4. 3.

S. BERNARDI QUAEDAM.

Vellum, 12 × 8, ff. 211.   Cent. xiii.

1.	S. Bernardus de consideratione	f. 1
	„ de amore dei	
2.	Sermo magistri Sertonis de iusto homine bene uiuente . .	46
3.	Bernardi Homiliae xlviii	59 b

On the fly-leaf is : Liber Mag. Ricardi Hopton quem emit ab
executoribus Petri Bylton pro xx s.   Hopton was Fellow of Eton
in 1453, and Rector of St Alban's, Wood-street, in 1477.

40. Bk. 4. 4.

EVANGELIA SLAVONICA.

Paper, 11¼ × 8½, ff. 289, 19 lines to a page, cent. xv.   In quires
of 8 ; there remain quires Γ 1 to ΛΘ 1 mutilated at beginning and
end.   The Gospels are followed by 13 leaves of synaxarion.   There
is an Italian note on the last page, too much mutilated to be read.

41. Bk. 4. 5.

HOMILIAE IN EVANGELIA.

Vellum, 10⅞ × 7¼, ff. 210, 27 and 34 lines to a page.   Cent. xi.
Probably written in Italy, but brought to England before Wotton's
time, if we may judge by the tables of contents, which may be of
cent. xv., xvi.   There are two of these.

In quires of eight leaves.

Contents :

xcii. Homilies on various Sunday and Festival Gospels.

Hom. 1 begins :

In illo tempore.   Cum appropinquasset dominus ihesus hierosolimis et venisset
bethfage...Ite in castellum et reliqua.   Spiritualiter autem duo discipuli qui in castellum
mittuntur, duos ordines significat predicatorum quorum unus ad iudeorum populum...

At the end of quire xvii in red on the lower margin : Gira
quaternionem in aña ✚ : and in a later hand : Require in octauo
folio ·xlviij· post.   At the place indicated is a rubric : ✚ et hoc est
adhuc de passione.

[C. M. A. 79.]

42. Bk. 4. 6.

[S. JOHANNIS CHRYSOSTOMI] OPUS IMPERFECTUM IN MATTHEUM.

Vellum, 10 × 7, ff. 311, 29 lines to a page. Cent. xv. Binding H.V. Fly-leaf at end from a service-book with music, containing an antiphon for Epiphany.

On f. 297 is this colophon :

Expliciunt omelie Iohannis Crisostomi patriarche constantinopolitani super Matheum operis imperfecti etc. Quod Wodewarde.

An index rerum in two hands follows on f. 297 b.

At the beginning :

Liber Collegii Regalis beate Marie de Eton ex dono magistri Thome Weston socii euisdem collegii xxiii° die Aprilis anno domini m° ccccliii° et anno Regni Regis Henrici Sexti xxxi°.

At the end :

Eton E. C. (or I. C.)

Ex dono magistri Willelmi Wey quondam socii istius collegii regalis beatissime marie de Eton.

[C. M. A. 80.]

43. Bk. 4. 7.

GLOSSA IN MATTHEUM.

Vellum, 10¼ × 7⅜, ff. 88, quires of 8 leaves, numbered i–xi : text and gloss. Cent. xiii. The gloss is followed by a list of S. Augustine's works. On a fly-leaf at the beginning is written the Sibylline acrostic on the last judgment. On one at the end is a receipt for making azorium.

At the beginning is :

Hic liber est Canonicorum de Otteham. This is the Premonstratensian house of Hottheham near Hailsham in Sussex, removed in cent. xiii. to Bayham.

[C. M. A. 60.]

44. Bk. 4. 8.

ALBERTUS MAGNUS IN LUCAM ET MARCUM.

Paper, 12 × 8½, ff. 624, in quires of 24 leaves, 33 lines to a page, in many hands. Cent. xv.

Albertus in Lucam	f. 1
,, in Marcum	481

At the end in a hand of cent. xv. or xvi. is Ihc mercy ladi help.
Many of the quires are signed, presumably by their scribes, thus :

f. 49	My3hel.
265	Martyn.
289	Wylkyn.
337	Cooper.
409	Bacon.
505	Wymarke [1].
529	Chambyr.
553	Bacon.
577	Churche.
601	Howchyne.

Given by W. Horman.

[C. M. A. 3.]

45. Bk. 4. 9.

PETRI COMESTORIS HISTORIA SCHOLASTICA.

Vellum, $11\frac{1}{2} \times 8$, ff. 246, in quires of 12, 10, and 8 leaves : double
columns.   Cent. xiii.   In a fine hand : an initial on f. 1 has been
defaced.   At the end is, as usual, the epitaph of Petrus Comestor.

At the bottom of f. 1 is a monastic press-mark h. xvij. which
resembles those of Norwich or Chichester.

[C. M. A. 41.]

46. Bk. 4. 10.

S. AMBROSII QUAEDAM.

Vellum, $11 \times 7\frac{5}{8}$, ff. 306, in a Roman hand, with good initials.
Cent. xv.   In quires of 10 leaves.

S. Ambrosii Epistolae	f. 1
Idem de morte S. Satiri fratris siue de resurrectione . . .	228
Ejusdem oratio	264
Idem de incarnatione	269
Idem de spiritu sancto	284

Possibly given by Wotton.

[C. M. A. 8.]

---

[1] Edmund Wymarke or Umarke, a secular Chaplain, took the degree of Bachelor of
Canon Law, 8 July 1532, at Oxford.

47. Bk. 4. 11.

S. AUGUSTINI CONFESSIONES, ETC.

Vellum, 11¾ × 8, ff. 202, in quires of 12 leaves, 51 lines to a page. Cent. xv.

S. Augustinus de doctrina Christiana.
Eiusdem Confessiones.

Johannis Wodeford questio de adoracione ymaginum . . . f. 121
    ,,   ,,   contra Jo. Wicliffe de eukaristia.
    ,,   ,,   tractatulus de peregrinacione ad loca sancta et
  sanctorum reliquiarum ueneratione 128
Opinio et confessio domini Jo. Wycliff de sacramento altaris ut recitat eum doctor Nicolaus Radecliff de sancto Albano in libro suo qui incipit *Vniuersis christi fidelibus* c. 27 . . . 131
Notabilia excerpta de questionibus Doctoris Wodeford contra eosdem Wicliffistas de eadem diuinissima eukaristia . . . . 138 b
f. 144 is blank.
S. Augustini de cognitione uerae uitae. 145
Cassiodorii de institutione diuinarum litterarum excerptum *Rursum inquit potest occultum inueniri* . . . . . . 156 b
S. Augustini de utilitate credendi 157
    ,, de assumptione B. V. Mariae 166
    ,, de moribus ecclesiae contra Manicheos . . . 169
Index rerum . . . . 181 b
Questio secunda doctoris subtilis (i.e. Duns Scotus) de ueritate fidei nostrae super prologum primi libri sententiarum . . . 194 b
Excerpta S. Thomae contra gentiles . . . . . . 198 b

At the end is:

Liber magistri Johannis Malberthorp. Malberthorp or Mabelthorp gave two MSS. (vi. Lat. and ci. Lat.) to Lincoln College, of which he was a Fellow. He was Fellow of Eton in 1447.

[C. M. A. 22.]

48. Bk. 4. 12.

S. AUGUSTINI QUAEDAM.

Vellum, 11 × 7½, ff. 241, quires of 8 leaves. Cent. xii. and xiv. Two volumes in one.

I. 31 to 40 lines on a page. Early xiith cent., well written, ff. 96.

S. Augustini de adulterinis coniugiis . . . . . . f. 1
    ,, de natura et origine animae . . . . . 17 b
    ,, sermo arrianorum 55
    ,, contra arrianorum perfidiam 57
    ,, contra aduersarium legis et prophetarum . . . 69
    ,, de uera innocentia. Cent. xiii. 97

II.　In double columns of 49 to 51 lines each.　Cent. xiii., xiv. ff. 97–241.

Annotationes anonymi in varia sacrae scripturae loca.　Headed in red : Notule super Genesim.　Contains notes on Genesis, the Gospels, the Catholic Epistles, Jerome's prologue, Gen., Exod., Leuit., Judic., 1 Reg.

Inc. Materia Moysi in hoc opere est creatio mundi.　*Expl.* Secundus patruus qui Iacobum interfecit.

This part of the volume has this inscription :

Liber beate marie de Beluero.　Hunc librum dedit frater Willelmus de Beluero prior eiusdem ecclesie deo et beate Marie de Beluero quem qui alienauerit uel fraudem aliquam inde fecerit indignacionem dei incurrat : anima dicti Willelmi et anime omnium fidelium defunctorum requiescant in pace.　Amen.　There is a similar note on f. 144 *b*.　The house referred to is the Benedictine Priory of Belvoir in Lincolnshire, subject to S. Albans Abbey.

The whole volume is

donum Guilielmi Horman quondam socii huius contubernii.

[C. M. A. 21.]

49 to 73.　Bk. 5. 1–14.　Bl. 5. 1–11.

OPERA JOSEPHI BEAUMONT D.D.

Twenty-five quarto volumes, 11⅛ × 9.　Cent. xviii. : containing the Theological works of Joseph Beaumont, D.D., Regius Professor of Divinity (1674–1699) and Master of S. Peter's College, Cambridge (1663–1699), copied from his autographs at the expense of Thomas Richardson, D.D., Master of S. Peter's College (1699–1733) and Fellow of Eton.　Presented by Dr Richardson in 1732. Dr Beaumont's portrait is prefixed to Vol. i.

The works consist of :

1.　A Commentary on the Epistle to the Romans, in ten volumes.
2.　　　　 ”　　　　”　　　　”　　　　Colossians, in three volumes.
3.　　　　 ”　　　　”　Ecclesiastes, in three volumes.
4.　De Terminis Theologicis, in four volumes.
5.　In loca selecta, in four volumes.
6.　De Libertate Christiana xv Praelectiones contra Georg. Enjedinum, or Examen Eniedini, in one volume.

[C. M. A. *vac.*]

74. Bk. 6. 1.

POSTILLA JANUENSIS · S · JANUENSIS SERMONES DOMINICALES.

Vellum, $10\frac{1}{8} \times 7\frac{3}{8}$, ff. 150, in double columns. Cent. xv., in three hands. In quires of 12 leaves.

On the first and last leaf is: Pertinet ad magistrum Walterum Smyth: on f. 1 is: Christe caput gratum mihi des finemque beatum.

[C. M. A. 83.]

75. Bk. 6. 2.

PSALTERIUM CUM CANTICIS GRAECE.

Paper, $8\frac{3}{8} \times 6$, ff. 93, 26 lines to a page. Cent. xv. In quires of 16 leaves.

Ps. cli. occurs in the proper place. On f. 1 is:

Κλαυδίου τοῦ ἀγκανθηροῦ¹ κτῆμα.

at the end:

κ̄ε ῑυ χ̄ε υἱὲ τοῦ θ̄υ ἐλέησόν με τὸν ἁμαρτωλῶν.

[C. M. A. 108.]

76. Bk. 6. 3.

S. HIERONYMUS SUPER DANIELEM, ETC.

Vellum, $9\frac{1}{8} \times 6\frac{1}{4}$, ff. 40 + 92; two volumes in one. Cent. xii. and xv. In quires of 10 leaves.

    I. S. Hieronymus in Danielem. Cent. xii. Rubricated initials.
      Followed by the *Capitula* of a book on sacred numbers, and a slip of cent. xiii.
      on similar matter.
    II. 1. Barenguidus (Berengaudus) in Apocalypsim, cent. xv.: in double columns.
      2. On the women at the Sepulchre, cent. xv.: ff. 2, in double columns.

On the fly-leaf:

Eton. E. C. (or I. C.).

Ex dono Willelmi Wey quondam socii istius Collegii Regalis Etone. (See Bk. 4. 6.)

[C. M. A. 75 (?).]

¹ ?=Alcantieri.

77. Bk. 6. 4.

GLOSSA SUPER MATTHEUM.

Vellum, 9¼ × 6¾, ff. 88 in quires of 8 leaves: no initials. Cent. xiii.

The fly-leaves are of cent. xiv. One begins: *Pitagorici autem*, the other: *omnes homines naturam scire desiderant.*

The gloss begins: Fecit deus duo luminaria in firmamento celi. A note of provenance on f. 1 is erased: on f. 2 *b* is a large number (·18·) in red. The writing resembles that of part II. of Bk. 4. 12.

The book belonged to Kempston and has his inscription.

[C. M. A. 60 (?).]

78. Bk. 6. 5.

PSALTERIUM CUM CANTICIS ET HYMNIS.

Vellum, 10¼ × 8, ff. 161, 22 lines to a page. Cent. xiii.

I.   Kalendar .   .   .   .   f.   1
      Psalterium cum canticis   3
II. Hymni. *Inc.* O lux beata Trinitas   128
              Expl. Canticum de uirginibus. Non uocaberis
      ultra derelicta...desolata.

The Psalter is preceded by two leaves of a Kalendar in red, black, blue, green and gold. Two medallions have been cut out of the margin of each of these leaves: no doubt they represented the Zodiacal sign and the occupation of each month. The months which remain are March, April, November, December. Among English saints we find Elfege, Mellitus, Justus, Thomas (Becket), and Birinus. This points to Canterbury.

The first leaf of the Psalter, and the initials to Pss. xxvii., xl., liii., cii., cix. are gone: those to Pss. lxxxiii. *Exultate*, and xcvii. *Cantate*, are left and are of good character, though rather rough. In the *Litany* we find SS. Erasmus, Alphege, Salvius, Blasius, Pancras, Alban, Oswald, Aedmund, *Martyrs:* Augustine, Odo, Dunstane ii., Audoenus, Uulganus, Remigius, Cuthbert, Swithun, Furseus, Wilfrid, Paulinus, Romanus, Guthlac, Columban, Wandregisil, Edward (inserted later, Edmund of Canterbury, Yreneus, Wlfstan, Richard, Hugh, Bertinus, Anna, Julian, Ethilbert), *Confessors:* Baptildis, Aeldrida, Mildrida, Austroberta, Osýþa (inserted, Edburga), *Virgins.*

The Hymns have a good gold initial. The volume was given by Thos. Horne, Fellow, in 1713.

[C. M. A. *vac.*]

79. Bk. 6. 6.

PETRUS DE PALMA, ETC.

Vellum, 8¼ × 5½, ff. 88 (in quires of 12 leaves, and one of 4) + 36 (in quires of 10 leaves and one of 6). Cent. xv.

> I.   29 lines to a page.
>>   1.   Ex Rodulpho Flauiacensi in Leuiticum.   ff. 1, 2.
>>   2.   Postilla fratris Petri de Palma in Parabolas Salomonis.   ff. 1–86.
> II. Index, later, on 36 ff., 46 lines to a page.
>>   Excerpsit Guil. Hormannus, scripsit Darellus.

The volume is 'donum Guil. Horman.'

[C. M. A. 102.]

80. Bk. 6. 7.

S. HIERONYMI, ETC. QUAEDAM.

Vellum, 9 × 5½, ff. 138 (16 quires of 8 leaves, and one of 10), 23 lines to a page. Cent. xii., xiii. Binding H.V.

> 1.   S. Hieronymus contra Iouinianum   .   .   .   .   .   . f.   1
> 2.   The genealogy of Christ. *Tres sorores*, etc. .   .   .   .   . 133 *b*
> 3.   De notis litterarum: a cypher used by Brutus and Augustus: b is substituted for a, c for b, etc.
> 4.   An anthem with music. Iohannes autem...Quo audito...Ite dicite Iohanni.
> 5.   Some matter relating to music, with notes and memorial verses.
> 6.   A hymn to S. Katherine, without music. Aue uirginum gemma Katerina.

The volume belonged to William Barett and then to Will. Horman, who gave it to the College.

[C. M. A. 74.]

81. Bk. 6. 8.

S. Anselmi Dialogus, etc.

Vellum, 8¼ × 5½, ff. 42, quires of 8 and 4 leaves, 37 lines to a
page: good initials. Cent. xiii. Written in England, perhaps at
S. Albans.

S. Anselmi Dialogus	f. 1
Miscellaneous extracts	28
A Hymn *Prima uirtus suffragetur*, with space for music . .	33
S. Gregorii Cura Pastoralis	37

On the last leaf is 'post hunc librum minores collaciones.'

[C. M. A. 11.]

82. Bk. 6. 9.

Willelmi de Monte quaedam.

Vellum, 9¼ × 6¼, ff. 90 and slips inserted, in quires of 10 and
8 leaves, 36 lines to a page. Cent. xiv.

1.	Liber numeralis Willelmi de Monte (he was a Canon of Lincoln in 1330). It treats of sacred numbers up to twelve . . .	f. 1
2.	Table to the following tract	64 *b*
3.	Eiusdem liber similitudinum, with many notes and insertions .	66
4.	Miscellaneous extracts	88 *b*

This volume strongly resembles the Bury S. Edmund's books.

[C. M. A. 61.]

83. Bk. 6. 10.

Paschasius Radbertus, etc.

Vellum, 9 × 6, ff. 83 + 116, two volumes in one. Cent. xi., xii.
and xiii., xiv. Fly-leaves from a law MS. of cent. xiv. in two
columns.

I.	1.	Paschasius Radbertus de corpore et sanguine Domini . . (Capitula f. 1 *b*. Text f. 3 *a*.)	f. 1
	2.	Extracts from the Decretals on the primacy of Rome . .	75

ff. 83 in double columns of 26 lines each in a strange sloping
hand, on very rough vellum.

Collation : a¹⁰ b⁸–i⁸ k⁸⁺¹ : quires numbered i–viiii. Cent. xi., xii.

II. 1. Distinctiones argute : in alphabetical order.
     2. Notes on *Palma* and *Tabernaculum.* Cent. xv.

ff. 116, 40 lines to a page, quires of 8 and 6 leaves. Cent. xiii., xiv. Very like a Bury book.

[C. M. A. 104.]

84. Bk. 6. 11.

ALANI AEQUIVOCA AD HERMENGALDUM ABBATEM S. AEGIDII.

Vellum, 9⅞ × 6⅞, ff. 250 + 4 blank, quires of 10 leaves and one of 4, 34 lines to a page. Cent. xiv., xv. Fly-leaves from a Kalendar of cent. xiv. containing the months of Oct. and March, with names of English saints Paulinus, Wilfrid, David, Gregory 'Anglorum apostolus,' Cuthbert, Wulframnus. Binding pink vellum : has had a label on the side : the number 8Λ remains ; also the title Alanus IΛ. Perhaps from Reading.

[C. M. A. 12.]

85. Bk. 6. 12.

LEONIS BAPTISTAE ALBERTI (MANTUANI) BREUE COM-
PENDIUM DE COMPONENDA STATUA.

Paper, 10¼ × 7⅛, ff. 11 + 8 blank (a⁸ b⁶, and 5 fly-leaves of another paper): vellum wrapper. Cent. xvi. (1544). Has a scale and two diagrams.
Given by Wotton (?).

[C. M. A. 5.]

86. Bk. 6. 13.

CYRILLI ALEXANDRINI LEXICON GRAECE.

Paper, 10⅝ × 7¾, not paged. Cent. xvii. (1679).
A transcript from a MS. 'quinti abhinc saeculi' belonging to Jo. Ciampini at Rome. *Inc.* ἀασάμην. *Expl.* ᾦ.
Given by Edward Betham, Fellow, in 1775.

[C. M. A. *vac.*]

87. Bk. 6. 14.

PLAUTI COMOEDIAE OCTO.

Vellum, 10 × 6⅝, ff. 112 + 6 blank, quires of 10 leaves, the signatures (catchwords) marked by grotesques and ornaments; written in Italy. Cent. xv.

1. Epigramma Plauti.	6. Cassina.
2. Amphitruo.	7. Cistellaria.
3. Asinaria.	8. Epidicus.
4. Captiui.	9. Aulularia.
5. Curculio (Gurgulio).	10. Sedigiti uersus (cent. xvi.).

Each play has a good initial in white and gold. On the fly-leaf is :

'Emptus patauij dum studerem leg. 1456 idibus Ianuariis'

in Bernardo Bembo's hand. On f. 1 *b* the words *Codex bernardi bembi* have been partially erased.

No doubt given by Wotton.

[C. M. A. 116.]

88. Bk. 6. 15.

M. T. CICERONIS ARATEA CUM SCHOLIIS.

Paper, 9¼ × 6½, ff. 43 + 8 blank (i⁴ a⁴ b¹⁰—e¹⁰ f⁸), in a fine Italian hand. Cent. xv., xvi.

Fragmentum Arati cum a < rgu > mento nouiter repertum in Sicilia.

1. Praefatio : *Aratus quidem fuit athinodori patris filius* . . f.. 1
2. Prolegomena : *Hic est stellarum ordo utrorunque circulorum* . iv
3. M. T. Ciceronis Aratea, with marginal comment . . . v
4. Comment in prose : *Solem per se ipsum* xxvii

Ends abruptly on f. xlix....siquis. Plura deficiunt que propter uetustatem et quinternionum fractionem colligi nequaquam potuerunt.

No doubt from Wotton.

[C. M. A. 120.]

89. Bk. 6. 16.

L. Annaei Senecae opera.

Vellum, 10 × 6⅞, ff. 187, double columns. Cent. xiii.

Misbound. The collation is as follows : v^{12} vi^{12} vii^{12+1} xvii^8 xviii^{12} xix^{12} xx^2 viii^2 ix^{12}–xv^{12} xvi^{18} xx^{2+1} xxi^{2+1} $[xxii^6]$.

1. Seneca de beneficiis : *inc.* (l. iv.)...cius amamur. Tot arbusta
non uno modo frugifera. Quires v–vii . . . . f. 1
2. Naturales quaestiones. Quires xvii, xviii 38
3. De clementia. Quire xix 58
4. Epistolae Pauli et Senecae, with preface from Jerome. Quire
xx (?) 70
5. Epitaphium Senecae : 6 lines . . . . . . 71 *b*
6. Epistolae ad Lucilium, with *Capitula* prefixed. Quires viii–xvi 72
7. De copia uerborum ad Paulum. Quire xx 176
8. De casibus fortuitis. Quire xxi 179
9. Excerpta de epistolis Senecae. Primum argumentum composite
mentis...(*expl.*) quod per neglegentiam fit 182

Ff. 182–187 are in another hand.

[C. M. A. 114.]

90. Bk. 6. 17.

M. T. Ciceronis, etc., quaedam.

Vellum, 9 × 5½, ff. 123, 42 lines to the page. Quires of 8 leaves. Very rotten with damp. Cent. xiii. Original binding of white skin over boards now replaced by a new morocco binding.

Collation : a^8 b^8 (wants 4) c^6 (wants 4, 5, 6) d^8 e^8 f^8 g^8 (wants 8) h^8 i^6 k^8 (wants 1, 6, 7, 8) l^8 m^8 (wants 8 blank) n^8 o^8 (wants 4, 5) p^8 q^8 r^8 (wants 4, 5, 6).

M. T. Ciceronis Paradoxa . . . . f. 1
Laelius 5
Cato Maior. *Expl.*....horis impendente timeris quis
(c. 67) . . . . 12 *b*
De Officiis 19
Epitaphium Ciceronis per xii sapientes . . . 48 *b*
Supra Tullium de amicitia 49
de senectute.
de paradoxis.
de officiis.
Ciceronis Timaeus Platonis. *Expl.* admonitione perspicio . . 50
Two blank leaves with late scribblings 62
Marcianus Capella de nuptiis Philologiae et Mercurii . . . 64
Inc. (l. i. p. 4 ed. Grotius) *crepi*tacula tinnitusque—ipsum to*nant. m*
(p. 17).

Liber ii. *Expl.* plenitudo (p. 26).
Followed by Liber viii. Astrologia Marciani, complete.
Macrobius de Somnio Scipionis, with diagrams . . . . f. 83
Liber ii. *Expl.* sonorum de re acumen emittit.

Many medical receipts of cent. xvii. are scribbled on the margins. On f. 1 is: Iste liber est de communitate...ha*u*erford...hug' de thoresby. It subsequently belonged to W. Bathon. (Laud), and was given to the College by Thos. Richardson, Fellow, in 1722.

[C. M. A. *vac.*]

91.   Bk. 6. 18.

P. OVIDII NASONIS OPERA.

Vellum, 10¾ × 7¾, ff. 169, double columns of 49 lines each. Rubricated initials. Cent. xiii., xiv.

Collation: i¹²–vi (numbered vii)¹² a¹² b¹² c¹²–e¹² viii¹² ix¹² (x)² wanting the last leaf blank.

Heroides	f. 1 *a*
Amores	18 *a*
De arte amandi	30 *b*
Remedia amoris	42 *b*
Nux	46 *b*
De sompnio siue Rosa	47 *b*
De pulice	48 *a*
De Cuculo	48 *a*
Fasti (with Kalendar on f. 72)	49 *a*
Metamorphoses	73 *a*
Tristia	135 *a*
Epistolae ex Ponto	153 *a*
De mirabilibus mundi	169 *a*

On f. 1 is 'liber vii^mus.

Liber collegii beate Marie prope Winton ex liberalitate...propicietur deus Amen.'

On the fly-leaf:

1695
Liber collegii Regalis Beatae Mariae de Eton ex dono Domini...(*sic*) Moyle.

Also, Barth. van Wouw; and

Iohannes Pabage his booke ex dono patrui Willelmi Pabage Maii die 7. 1602.

The order of owners is most likely: Winchester, Pabage, van Wouw, Moyle. See Shuckburgh's Heroides of Ovid.

[C. M. A. *vac.*]

92 to 95. Bl. 1. 1, 2, 3, 4.

Paper, 12¼ × 13½. Sec. xvi. (1541).

A work in four volumes, which must be described separately. The history of the whole set appears from the following notices in the binding :

"This, with the three following volumes, was given me by the Right Honble the Lord Viscount Palmerston 'Et vero et magno dignum est hoc munus amico' [signed] R. Ellys."

After his death they were returned to Lord Palmerston by the then Lady Ellys, relict of Sir Richard Ellys; and by him presented to the College in 1750 (Apr. 26), as we learn from a printed label pasted in each volume.

Hanc Insignium Gentilitiorum et Imaginum seriem admirandam, a primis usque temporibus deductam, Artis Graphicae coloribus pulcherrime illuminatam, et quatuor voluminibus descriptam, Antiquitatum Historicarum Monumentum pretiosum, Henricus Temple Vicecomes de Palmerston In Schola Etonensi aliquando Discipulus, et Coll. Regal. Cantab. Soc. Commensalis pro singulari erga Etonenses suos Benevolentia D.D. Apr. 26 MDCCL.

On the fly-leaf are two distichs by Maittaire :

> Debuit et voluit sic pingi Roma triumphans
> Dignus Romano est hic color imperio.
>
> M. Maittaire.
>
> Quantum Roma inter cunctas caput extulit urbes
> Tantum hoc præ cunctis grande refulget opus.
>
> Id.

Vol. I. is Joannis Tirolli Antiquitates, ff. 220. The author was Respublice Augustane aedificiorum publicorum prefectus.

Contents of Vol. I.

1. Index.

2. Verso of last leaf of index. Sententia Heroaldi Joannes Tirollus, etc. He is represented standing on a pedestal, with gold mace and tabard, and laurel wreath; his arm raised ; his scutcheon by him.

3. Next page, the Dedication to Henry VIII., with the arms of England supported by two griffins, two roses, crown, and garter. *Verso.* Dedication continued. The work was done at the expense of Jacobus Hörproth, Reipublicae Augustanae consul, etc., whose scutcheon is appended.

4. f. 1. In capitals. 'Omnis caro corrupit viam suam ideo Dei ira exarsit et disperdit omnem carnem diluvio, pium vero Noe cum animabus octo tantum servavit ut in Gene: viii. et ix. cap. scribitur...Ordine regna inde ab Noe ad Romanum usque invenies, ad Romulum et Remum, deinde ad senatum Romanum vsque, deinde a primo Imperatore Julio ad Carolum usque V. omnia hec ordine conscripta in graciam invictissimi

E. MSS.

Imperatoris Caroli V. omniumque imperatorum sibi succedencium • Deo • O. M. gloria et honor in perpetuum.   Amen.'

f. 1 *b*, 2 *a*.   The same, in German rhyme.

f. 3 *a*.   Archa Noe.   A full-page drawing, coloured, and heightened with gold.   The ark in the midst.   Noah at the window.   In the pediment of the ark is a carving of God the Father.

f. 4 *a*.   Sem and his descendants building.   A full-page painting.

f. 5 *a*.   Cham. ⎫
f. 7 *a*.   Japhet. ⎬ Similar paintings.

f. 8 *a*.   Nemroth and the tower of Babel.

8 *b*.   The shield of Assur.

9 *a*.   Half-length.   Belus, with shield, and a devil on a pillar by him.

9 *b*.   Ninus.

10 *a*.   Ninius about to stab Semiramis.   Other pictures of Assyrian kings.

13 *a*.   Tartars.   Full-page.   Bleeding heads are brought to a chief, and wine is poured into one of them.

15 *a*.   Half-length.   Solyman with dart.

16 *b*.   A battle with amazons.

19 *b*.   Prester John seated on a throne with 12 lions on the steps.   Courtiers and kings round him.   Subject monarchs are seen in the landscape, throned, in various parts.

24 *a*.   A Soldan using a king as his horse-block.

After f. 30 are 2 ff., not numbered, with full-length pictures of the Emperor of the East, and of the West.

31 *b*.   A Herald.

32 *b*.   In capitals.   Introduction to the Roman Empire.

ff. 34–6 are gone.   No doubt they contained the glory of Romulus and Remus.

ff. 37 sqq. have full-length portraits of the Roman kings, beginning with Numa. Each has some distinguishing mark by him on the pedestal on which he stands; e.g.

39 *a*.   Ancus Martius has beside him : on *L*. a peasant with whip, hat, boots, etc., borrows money from a man seated at a table : on *R*. the same peasant, bareheaded and barelegged, sits in the stocks; his hands and legs (below the knee) confined.   The stocks are three beams with padlocks attached.   This alludes to Ancus's Laws for Debt.

f. 40 is a folded sheet of vellum, and has a large painting of the Triumph of L. Tarquinius Priscus over the Etruscans.   On a standard is the date 1541.

f. 42 is a similar sheet.   On it is, on *R*. above, Lucretia attacked by Sextus.   Below, her death, her funeral, and the people swearing to expel the kings.   On *L*. is a battle the battle of Lake Regillus.

f. 43.   A Herald.

44 *b*, 45 *a*.   Across the page.   The Institution of Military Tribunes.

46 *a*.   A Praetor, judging.

47 *a*.   Senators.

48 *a*.   Two Consuls, in Doctors' gowns and caps.

49 *a*.   A Proconsul, with lictors.

50 *a*.   A Dictator in a blue high hat, with a naked sword.

51 *a*.   Decemviri sitting.

52 *a*.   Tribuni plebis, under a tree.

53 *a*.   Censors at their work.

54 *a*. Three Military Tribunes under an umbrella-like canopy.

55 *a*. Praefecti Annonae in a Rathhaus painted outside with hunting-scenes.

56 *a*. Aediles.

57 *b*. Standards.

58 *b*. Eagles. One is crowned, and smaller birds do homage to it: one flies toward the sun, another on a rock pushes a young one out of the nest. One attacks a stag, and one a dragon in a cave.

62 *a*. Julius Caesar full-length, and so on with the whole series of Emperors.

93 *b*. A herald, pointing to

94 *a* sqq. The 'Thirty Tyrants,' two on a page. Cyriades has a large tabby cat by him.

102. The series continues with Claudius II.

141 *b*. Carolus Magnus.

142 *b*, 143 *a*. Census of the Peers of Charlemagne, etc.

155 *a*. Under architecture, the arms of Mecklenburg, as 'archicamera regni.'

158 *b*, 159 *a*. The Four Dukes and Four Margraves of the Empire.

160 *b*, 161 *a*. The Four Landgraves and Four Burgraves and Four 'Comites Majores.'

212 *a*. On a folding sheet of vellum Fredericus M. *Label*, AEIOV.

212 *b*. The double-headed eagle with the shields of all the provinces upon it.

213 *a*. A vellum sheet. 1. Maximilian.   *Label*, 'Halt masz.'
　　　　　　　　　　　　　2. Carolus V. (1529). *Label*, 'Plus ultra.'

213 *b*. A great eagle with shields upon it.

215. 1. The Columns of Hercules with *Scrolls*, 'Plus ultra.'
　　　　2. Ferdinand (1530).

216. Two great eagles, with shields shewing the extent of the Empire under Charles V. and Ferdinand.

Voll. II. III. IV. contain a further work by J. Tirollus:

'De nobilitate et ortu heroum.'

Bl. 1. 2, and 4 are paged consecutively and contain together ff. 413. They consist of woodcut outlines blazoned in colours (but not all finished) of the arms of German Nobles, with text in Latin and German.

Bl. 1. 3 contains ff. 203 and has the painted arms of all the foreign states.

96. Bl. 1. 5.

PETRI PICTAVENSIS COMPENDIUM VETERIS TESTAMENTI.

Vellum, $18\frac{1}{2} \times 13\frac{3}{4}$, ff. 23, sec. xiii. (cir. 1244).

Incipit compendium ueteris testamenti editum a magistro petro pictauensi et cancellario parisiensi.

It is a short Universal Chronicle extending from the Creation to 1244 A.D., illustrated with medallions and genealogies.

The following are the *figured* medallions:

f. 1 *a.*   A circle divided into three parts: above is Christ and two angels below Him. Below on *L.* the Fall, with human-headed serpent; on *R.* the Expulsion.

Heads of Delbora and Calmana, the sisters of Cain and Abel.

1 *b.*   *Enoch.*   A hand proceeding from clouds takes his hand.

　　　Lamech.   With bow and arrow.

　　　Noe.   With axe.

　　　Two plans of the ark, one with people and animals in it.

f. 2 is gone.

f. 3 *a* (iiij).   Heads of *Booz, Ruth,* and some of the Judges.

3 *b.*   *Saul* seated as king.

4 *a.*   Unction of David.

　　　Salomon holding the temple.

4 *b.*   Some heads of kings.

5 *a.*   Heads of kings.   *Athalia* as a man.

5 *b.*   *Manasses* holding a saw (with which he put Isaiah to death).

7 *a.*   The rapture of *Abacuc* (see 'Bel and the Dragon') with reapers.

　　　Darius throned full-face; a larger drawing.

7 *b.*   *Judith* beheading *Holofernes.*

　　　A plan of Jerusalem.

8 *a.*   Larger drawing.   *Esther* and *Mardocheus* talk to *Aman.*

　　　L. Mardocheus mounted.

　　　R. Aman hanging to a tree.

8 *b.*   *Alexander* seated full-face, with sword.

9 *a.*   *Judas Machabeus* on horseback.

　　　Pompeius seated.

9 *b.*   *Julius Caesar* as king.

　　　Joseph (the carpenter) seated.

f. 10 cut out.

f. 10 (11) *a.*   Heads of Emperors and Popes.

　　　　　Otho stabs himself.

　　　　　Vespasianus holds a head on a sword.

　　　　　Tytus gives a ring to a man.

10 *b.*   Pope *S. Alexander* with aspergillum and bucket (as having instituted holy water).

　　　S. Ignatius, a seraph singing above him; in allusion to the vision which led to the practice of antiphonal singing in churches.

11 *a.*   *Galenus* holding a wide-mouthed vessel.

12 *a.*   *S. Paulus Heremita* with crutch.

12 *b.*   *Diocletianus,* a devil at his ear (as persecutor).

　　　S. Helena seated.

　　　S. Nicholaus as Bishop: full-length.

f. 15 *a.*   *Justinianus* looks at his right hand.

15 *b.*   *S. Medardus,* the medallion cut out.

16 *b.*   *Mahumet,* a devil coming out of his mouth.

19 *a.*   S. Alphege, with head bleeding, and mitre falling off.

20 *a.*   *Robertus curta area* in mail.

20 *b.*   *Bernardus abbas,* half-length, with pastoral staff.

21 a. Martyrdom of S. Thomas of Canterbury. The four knights; one wounds Grim's arm.

Richard I. in mail.

21 b. John... A Bishop bleeding.

S. Dominic, full length, with staff and wallet.

22 a. S. Francis preaching to three birds; *frater iohannes* sits and listens.

On f. 7 a is the name 'Elizabeth Flobern' in a hand of sec. xvii.

[C. M. A. *vac.*]

97. Bl. i. 6.

Decreta Romanorum Pontificum, etc.

Vellum, 17 × 12¾, ff. 370, in double columns of 44 lines each. Cent. xii. The hand is very fine, possibly French.

Collation: in quires of 8 leaves, numbered i–xlvi, the xlviith is of 4 leaves, 1–3 blank, the 4th attached to the cover.

Contents:

Index (of cent. xv.)	f. i
Nomina xi Regionum	ii
Praefatio Isidori	1
Aurelii Carthaginensis Episcopi Epistola ad Damasum . . .	2 b
Damasi rescriptum	2 b
Decreta Romanorum Pontificum (from Clement to Nicholas I.) .	7 b
Concilia (from Nicaenum to Hispalense secundum) . . .	234

The title, in capitals, is magnificent, and the initials, usually in red on green, very bold. There are marginal notes of cent. xv. The fly-leaves are from a Concordance of cent. xv.

On the first page is a title of cent. xv.:

Liber Decretorum Roman. Pontif. et incipit in 2° fo. *tes viij.*

A chain-mark is visible on the top *R.* corner of the first leaves: there is also a rust-mark in the centre, shewing that the book had formerly the strap and pin fastening.

[C. M. A. 47.]

98. Bl. 1. 7.

WILL. LYNDEWODE PROVINCIALE.

Vellum, 16 × 11⅛, ff. 314 + 34, in double columns of 56 lines each. Cent. xv. English writing. In quires of ten leaves.

The contents, preceded by a table, consist of Constitutions of the Archbishops of Canterbury from Stephen Langton to Henry Chichele. Then follow the *Liber penitentialis* and an Index: and lastly, some supplementary constitutions, ending with one of Abp Stratford in 1445.

At the beginning of the text is the inscription: *Assit principio sancta maria meo.*

The book was given by Will. Horman.

On the last fly-leaf are several scribbles, e.g.

> Will^mi Linwode super prouintialibus,

and

> Willelmus Butler ẏs a knaue.

On the first fly-leaf:

> Karulus Thornhyll
> Willelmus Butler
> Radulfus fferysig (?) decanus
> Radulfus Goth archidiaconus;

and five lines from an English version of Mapes's *Apocalypsis Goliae,* beginning

> Ther was ye deyn and ye offycyall
> W^t ij fayces lyke a dyall....

[C. M. A. 90.]

99. Bl. 1. 8.

SECUNDA PARS CATHALOGI SANCTORUM PETRI DE NATALIBUS.

Vellum, 15⅝ × 12¼, ff. 220 + Index, in double columns of 58 lines each. French writing (?). Cent. xiv.

In quires of 8 leaves. The binding is original, of stamped leather over boards. The title, '2ª pars Cathalogi Sanctorum,' is on the last cover, formerly protected by a slip of horn.

The donor's name has been erased. We can read :

ex dono magistri ...ags (?) socii istius collegii.

Below it is $\overset{\frown}{\text{E C}}$ (or $\overset{\frown}{\text{I C}}$), which is a mark characteristic of William Wey.

The contents extend from the Conversion of S. Paul (Jan. 25) to SS. Flora and Lucilla, VV. and MM. (July 29).

Fol. 1 has a good initial and border of small leaf-work : a note of cent. xvii. attributes the work to Jac. de Voragine, or Petrus de Natalibus.

[C. M. A. 124.]

100. Bl. 1. 9.

S. JUSTINI MARTYRIS, ETC., QUAEDAM GRAECE.

Paper, $12\frac{5}{8} \times 9$, ff. 70, 31 lines to a page. Cent. xvi. (1534).
Collation : a⁸ bc¹⁰ d⁴ e⁶–g⁶ h¹⁰ i¹⁰.

Contents :

S. Justini Martyris Epistola ad Zenonem et Serenam	. . .	f. 1
Athenagorae Legatio pro Christianis	. . . . . .	8
Idem De Resurrectione .	. . . .	34
Tatiani Oratio ad Graecos	. . . .	52

There are marginal notes in Greek and Latin.

The colophon at the end gives the scribe's name, Valeriano of Forli :

Οὐαλεριανὸς Φορολιβιεὺς ὁ ᾿Αλβίνου κανονικὸς τοῦ πολίτου τοῦ σωτῆρος ταύτην ἔγραψε βίβλον 1534.

The MS. has been investigated by Gebhardt and Harnack. Their results may be seen in *Texte u. Untersuchungen*, I. pp. 4–6, 68, etc. All MSS. of the apologetic works of Justin, Athenagoras and Tatian go back to the Parisian MS. 451, written by Baanes for Arethas of Caesarea (A.D. 914).

This Eton MS. is a copy of one at Bologna (plut. xxii.). The scribe is not unknown. He is mentioned by Gardthausen (*Griechische Paläographie*, p. 341) and Graux (*Essai sur les origines du fond grec de l'Escurial*, pp. 189, 267).

CATALOGUE OF MSS.

This MS. was used by William Worth for his edition of Tatian, Oxford, 1700, and Dechair's Athenagoras, 1706: it was collated twice for Otto, the second time by Dr Gwynne.

It was no doubt given by Wotton.

[C. M. A. 88.]

101. Bl. 1. 10.

SS. AUGUSTINI ET GREGORII QUAEDAM.

Vellum, 14⅞ × 10⅝, ff. 181 + 157, two volumes in one. Cent. xiv. and xv. Binding H.V.

Part I. S. Augustini in Ioannem tractatus cxxiv.

Cent. xv.: in double columns of 49 lines each. The first page is bordered.

Collation: 1⁸–22⁸ 23⁴ (+ 1): 181 leaves.

Part II. S. Gregorii Magni

Homiliae xl.
Homiliae in Ezechielem.
De Cura Pastorali ('Pastoralia').
Dialogorum libri iv.

Of cent. xiv.

Collation: 1¹ 2¹²–13¹² 14¹⁴ = 157 leaves.

The following note applies to Part II. of this book only:

Istum librum ego Magister Petrus hopton emi ab executore petri Bylton pro lvj s viij di aᵒ dⁿⁱ mᵒ ccccᵒ lvᵒ.

[C. M. A. 17.]

102. Bl. 2. 1.

NIC. GORRANUS SUPER LUCAM.

Vellum, 15½ × 10¼, ff. 255, 52 lines to a page. Cent. xv. (1450). Flemish writing (?), not beautiful. There is a good initial at the beginning. Binding H.V.: in quires of eight leaves.

Contents:

1. Nicholaus Gorranus († 1295) de ordine predicatorum super Lucam.
2. Index rerum in double columns.

Colophon:

Explicit opus super euangelium Luce per egregium doctorem mag. Nich. Gorram ordinis predicatorum. Scriptum anno 1450.

> Sit propter scripta semper trinitas benedicta
> Hunc que letificet qui mihi bona prebet.

A monogram follows, **W** and **G** being the principal letters, and below it are the words ' per cistolam.'

[C. M. A. 62.]

103. Bl. 2. 2.

NIC. GORRANUS SUPER EPISTOLAS.

Vellum, 14½ × 10½, ff. 134, in double columns of 45 lines each. Cent. xv. Dutch writing (?): a fine hand.

Collation: a⁸–r⁸ (7, 8 cancelled).

Contents:

Nic. Gorranus super i. ii. Epist. ad Timotheum.
        ,, Epist. ad Titum.
        ,,   ,,   Philemonem.
        ,,   ,,   Hebreos.

Fol. 1 is bordered, and has medallions at the corners, two of Paschal Lambs and two of Eagles.

The MS. belonged to S. Alban's Abbey. At the end this notice has been added:

Hunc librum ad usum conventus monasterii Sc̄i Albani assignavit venerabilis pater dominus Johannes Whethamstede olim abbas monasterii antedicti, vinculoque anathematis innodavit illos omnes qui aut titulum illius delere curaverint aut ad usus applicare presumpserint alienos.

There is a chain-mark at the right lower corner of the front cover.

[C. M. A. 64.]

104. Bl. 2. 3.

HUGO DE VIENNA SUPER XI EPISTOLAS PAULI.

Vellum, 15¼ × 10, ff. 279. Cent. xv. English writing. Binding H.V.; fly-leaves from Concordance.

Collation : a⁶ (wants 1) b⁸–z⁸ aa⁸–mm⁸ nn².

Contents :

Hugo de Vienna super Epistolas Pauli (viz. Gal., Eph., Phil., Col., i. ii. Thess., i. ii. Tim., Tit., Philem., Hebr.).

At the beginning of each Epistle is a fine initial and partial border : at the beginning of Galatians is a larger border and two good initials.

[C. M. A. 82.]

105. Bl. 2. 4.

S. AUGUSTINI EPISTOLAE, ETC.

Vellum, 14¾ × 10½, ff. 179, in double columns of 40 lines each. Cent. xii., xiii. The writing and initials are good. There is a chain-mark at right of front cover, at bottom.

Collation : a⁴ (4 cancelled) i⁸–xxii⁸.

Contents :

Table . . . . f.	i *b*
S. Augustini Epistolae	1
Sermones duo (i) de uita et moribus clericorum . .	172
(ii) excusatorius pro clericis . . .	174
Adnotatio ad Ep. liv	176

On the fly-leaf are these entries :

Liber mag. Thome Mareys Rectoris de Stormouth in comitatu Kantie emptus de executoribus Thome Chycheley archidiaconi Cantuariensis anno dⁿⁱ 1468° vltimo die mensis Aprilis.

Liber mag. Joh. Mocer vicarii de tenterden emptus cantuarie ab executoribus mag. Thome maris et a mag. Simone hogges officiali pro 33 s 4 di.

[C. M. A. 16.]

106. Bl. 2. 5.

S. AUGUSTINI SERMONES, ETC.

Vellum, 15¼ × 11¼, ff. 139, in double columns of 47 lines each. Cent. xi., xii. and xv. Well written, with some good initials. Binding H.V.: fly-leaves from Concordance. Chain-mark lower right corner, in front.

Collation: a² b⁴ (1, 2 cancelled) i⁸–viii⁸ ‖ ix⁸–xiv⁸ xv⁸ (6 cancelled) xvi⁸ xvii⁴ (4 cancelled) c⁶ (6 cancelled).

Contents:

S. Augustini Regula　.　.　.　.　.　.　.　.　.　f. i
S. Hieronymi Sermo de omnipotentia　.　.　.　.　.　.　iii
Tabula　.　.　.　.　.　.　.　.　.　.　.　.　.　i
S. Augustini Sermones de uerbis domini.
　　　　　　　　　　de uerbis apostoli.
　　　　　　　　　　de actis apostolorum.
　　　　　　　　　　super epistolas canonicas.
　　　　　　　　　　duo pro defunctis.
S. Augustini Vita.
Index of cent. xv.

The Sermon of S. Jerome is on two inserted leaves of cent. xv. of smaller size after f. ii.

On f. 1 *a* is:

　　　　Vnde supperbimus, quid ego, quid tu, nisi fimus
　　　　primus homo limus, sortem mutare nequimus.

Before the life of S. Augustine:

　　　　Est labor est finis requies menti data binis
　　　　Indita mandatis capiatur sumite gratis.

At the end of quire viii, about one-third of a column is left blank, but the text has no gap.

The MS. is 'donum M. Johannis moyer': probably the Johannes Mocer of no. 105.

　　　　　　　　　　　　　　　　[C. M. A. 19.]

107.　Bl. 2. 6.

S. Augustinus de Ciuitate Dei.

Vellum, 15¾ × 10¾, ff. 227, in double columns of 46 lines each. Cent. xiii., in a good hand. The fly-leaves from a MS. of cent. xv. Binding, stamped leather, with four-fold diagonal lines intersecting: chain-mark at right lower corner in front.

Collation: i¹⁰–xx¹⁰ xxi¹² xxii¹² xxiii⁴ (4 attached to cover).

Contents:

Capitula　.　.　.　.　.　.　.　.　.　.　.　f. i
Prologus　.　.　.　.　.　.　.　.　.　.　.　v *b*
S. Augustinus de Ciuitate Dei　.　.　.　.　.　.　.　vi

On f. vi is an initial, with gold ground, representing S. Augustine vested as a Bishop, writing at a desk: there are good decorative initials throughout.

[C. M. A. 18.]

108. Bl. 2. 7.

S. AUGUSTINI ET NIC. DE LYRA QUAEDAM.

Vellum, $13\frac{1}{4} \times 9$, ff. 111 + 108, two volumes bound in one. Cent. xiv. and xv. (1403). Binding and chain-mark as the last: fly-leaves from a MS. of cent. xv. (law).

Contents:

I. S. Augustinus de Trinitate. Cent. xiv.

In double columns of 40 lines each: the hand has an Italian look, but is most likely English: floriated initials. Fol. 1 is mutilated.

Collation: 1^{12}–9^{12} 10^4 (1 cancelled).

II. 1. Tabula in Nic. de Lyra. Cent. xv.

In double columns of 47 lines each: fol. 1 is bordered: the hand gets larger towards the end.

Collation: a^{12} b^8–g^8 h^6 (6 cancelled) i^{10} k^{12} (12 cancelled) l^{10} (10 cancelled) m^{12} n^4 (4 cancelled) o^2.

Colophon:

Explicit tabula super doctore de lyra compilata et scripta per fratrem Willelmum Morton de sacro ordine fratrum minorum in conuentu Couentrey anno domini m⁰ cccc^{mo} tercio.

2. Questiones Lyrae super biblia. Cent. xv. ff. 2.

At the end is this note:

Nota quod iste doctor de lira fecit tria quodlibeta: primum est contra quendam iudeum ex verbis euangelij contra Christum nequiter arguentem: 2^m quodlibetum est contra iudeos de aduentis messie et 3^m est de visione beata: et ista tria quodlibeta habentur in quodam libro in collegio lincoln. oxon. et liber erat datus per doctorem Gasthoñ (i.e. Gascoigne) predicto collegio ut claret in eodem libro ibid.

The MS. alluded to is apparently no longer at Lincoln College.

[C. M. A. 15.]

109. Bl. 2. 8.

RUFFINI HISTORIA ECCLESIASTICA, ETC.

Vellum, $15\frac{1}{4} \times 11\frac{1}{4}$, ff. 186, in double columns. Cent. xiii. Binding H.V.: chain-mark lower *R.* front.

Collation : i⁸–x⁸ ‖ xi⁸–xiii⁸ | xiiii⁸–xxiii⁸ xxiiii².

Contents :

    1. Ruffini Aquileiensis Historiae Ecclesiasticae libri xi.   . . f. 1

There is a fine initial to the prologue : and the initials throughout are coloured.

    2. Vita B. Wulurici anachorete Haselbergie († 1154) per ven. Joh.
        priorem de Forda ad dom. Barthol. Exoniensem Episcopum f. 81

In two books. There are two prologues, (*a*) to Bartholomew Bp of Exeter, (*b*) to Baldwin Abp of Canterbury.

There are other MSS. of this Life, for which see Sir T. Duffus Hardy's *Catalogue of Materials*, Vol. II. p. 267, who does not mention this MS.: a xiith century MS. recently acquired by the University Library at Cambridge (Add. 3037) should also be added to the list.

S. Wuluric lived at Haselbury in Herefordshire.

    3. Robertus Miledunensis Episcopus Herfordensis Anglus de
        Sacramentis Veteris et Noui Testamenti, de incarnatione
        Christi et aliis . . . . f. 105

In another hand. The author died in 1166.

[C. M. A. 120.]

110. Bl. 2. 9.

L. ANNAEI SENECAE TRAGOEDIAE.

Vellum, $15\frac{5}{8} \times 10\frac{1}{2}$, ff. 52 + 4 fly-leaves, in three and two columns on a page, of 56 lines each. Cent. xiii. Italian writing.

Collation : a⁸–f⁸ g⁴.

Contents :

    L. Annaei Senecae Hercules Furens . . . . . . f. 1
               Thyestes 5
               Thebais . . . . 10 *b*

L. Annaei Senecae Hippolytus	13 *b*
Oedipus	19
Troades	24
Medea	29 *b*
Agamemnon	34
Octavia	38 *b*
Hercules Oetaeus	43

On f. 52 *b*, in three columns, is the tract *Omne peccatum est acti*, followed by four lines: 'Seneca Paulo.   Tulit priscorum aetas Macedonum,' etc.

The first seven pages are in triple columns: there are marginal notes in a later hand.   On f. 1 *b* is a note of the births of two children (family name not given) in 1391 and 1395: at the end are scribbles in Hebrew, and the following note:

hoc senece volumen tragiedalle (tragicale ?) quod meum est emi ego (name erased) ducatis quinque cum dimidio id est ducatis V+ quo tempore uinantie [cum] in domo eximij arcium ac theologogie (*sic*) doctoris magistri Johannis fromosigine morabar anno natiuitatis milesimo quadragintessimo quinquagessimo, anno Jubilei.

The MS. was no doubt given by Wotton.

[C. M. A. 113.]

111.   Bl. 2. 9* (olim Bo. 2. 7).

PROPOSITIONES EPISCOPORUM ANGLICANORUM GRAECE ET LATINE.

Paper, 13¼ × 9, pp. 93.   Cent. xviii.   Given by Edward Waddington, Bishop of Chichester, 1731.

Contents:

Προθέσεις τινες εἰς τὴν τῶν καθολικῶν καὶ ὀρθοδόξων τῆς ἐκκλησίας Βρεττανικῆς λειψάνων μετὰ τῆς Ἀνατολικῆς καθολικῆς καὶ Ἀποστολικῆς ἐκκλησίας συμφώνησιν.

Proposals for union addressed by the Nonjuring Bishops to the Greek Church: dated, London xv. Kal. Sept. 1716, and signed by

Jeremy Collier, Bishop,
Archibald Campbell, Bishop;

attested by:

John Sharp, D.D.,
Fra. Lee, M.R.C.S.

Followed by (2) the answer of the Orthodox Church, and (3) the reply of the Nonjuring Bishops, 29 May 1722: this last signed by the Scotch Bishops Archibald and James, and the English Bishops Jeremy and Thomas.

Followed by the account of the English Communion Office submitted by the Nonjurors to the Greek Church for approval.

In Greek and Latin: neatly transcribed.

[C. M. A. *vac.*]

112. Bl. 2. 10.

THE DIVINA COMMEDIA OF DANTE.

Vellum, $15\frac{1}{2} \times 10\frac{3}{4}$, ff. 84, in double columns of 45 lines each. Cent. xv.

Collation: a^{10} b^8 c^{10} || d^{10} e^8 f^{10} || g^{10} h^8 i^{10}.

Fol. 1 *a* is bordered: it has suffered from use: in the lower margin is a shield, quarterly *or* and *sable*, a fess *argent* (the arms of Dante).

The initial to *Canto* i. of the *Inferno* has a picture: Dante, in light blue and white, is following Virgil, bearded, in red, with cap, who looks back at him, and stands by a green rock (?). The ground is red.

The *Purgatorio* begins on f. 29: the first initial shews Dante and Virgil in a boat, pointing upwards and talking; the ground is red, the water green. One side of this page is bordered.

The *Paradiso* begins on f. 57: the first initial shews, on a red ground, Dante in blue, his arms crossed: on *R.*, higher up, Beatrice stands and points upward: part of a blue sphere is seen behind her: a border on one side of the page.

Each *canto* has a flourished initial.

On the last page has been a note in several lines, partially erased, beginning, ' Nota che questo Dante.......'

The MS. no doubt was given by Wotton.

It is denoted by the letter X in Moore's *Textual Criticism of the Divina Commedia*, where it is described (p. 549) and well spoken of. It is no. 484 in Colomb de Batines' list.

[C. M. A. 44.]

113. Bl. 2. 11.

HERODOTI HALICARNASSENSIS HISTORIA GRAECE.

Vellum, 16 × 10⅜, ff. 270 + 8 blank, 35 lines to a page.
Cent. xv.

Collation: a² 1¹⁰–27¹⁰ b⁶.

There are good rubricated ornaments at the beginnings of the
books: and marginal notes in Greek and Latin by both the
original scribe and a later hand.

On the first vellum fly-leaf has been a dedication, or letter,
occupying about 18 lines, now carefully erased.   The words *famulo
tuo* are legible at the end of line 1.

There has also been a line erased on the first page of the text,
and probably also a name written in Greek.

Doubtless given by Wotton.

[C. M. A. 73.]

114. Bl. 2. 12.

PETRI LOMBARDI SENTENTIARUM LIBRI IV.

Vellum, 14 × 9¾, ff. 280, in double columns of 34 lines each.
Cent. xiv.   Binding H.V.

Collation: 1¹²–7¹² 8⁶ ‖ 9¹²–17¹² 18⁶ ‖ 19¹²–24¹² 25⁴ (4 attached to
cover).

There are rubricated headings and coloured initials.

On f. 1 is:

Donum Richardi hopton sacre theologie professoris et quondam socij huius collegij.

The name Beaufort is written on f. 1 of text.

There are *capitula* to the several books, and marginal notes;
also notes at the end.

[C. M. A. 93.]

115. Bl. 3. 1 [formerly Bk. 3. 14].

COMMENTARY OF BENVENUTO DA IMOLA ON THE DIVINA COMMEDIA IN ITALIAN.

Paper, $11\frac{1}{2} \times 8\frac{1}{2}$, ff. 97, in double columns of 64 lines.   Cent. xv.

Incipit:

Nel mezo—vita ad intelligencia de la presente chomedia si chome usano li espositori in le scientie.

Collation: a¹⁴ b¹⁰–d¹⁰ e² (2 cancelled) ‖ f¹² g¹⁰–k¹⁰ (last 3 blank).

A former owner's name, Jo. Delphini, is on the fly-leaf.

No doubt given by Wotton.

[C. M. A. 45.]

116. Bl. 3. 2.

S. THOMAE AQUINATIS SUMMAE LIBER I.

Vellum, 13×9, ff. 153, in double columns of 52 lines each. Cent. xiv.

There is a good initial at the beginning.

Binding, fourfold diagonal lines intersecting : chain-mark lower *R*. front.

Collation: a¹²–m¹² n¹² (10–12 cancelled).

There is a Tabula, beginning on f. 149 *b*.

[C. M. A. 118.]

117. Bl. 3. 3.

ROBERTI GROSTHEDE DICTA, ETC.

Vellum, 13×9, ff. 98, in double columns.   Cent. xv.

Contents :

1. Dicta cxlvii Roberti Grosthede Episcopi Lincolniensis cum
    tabula   .   .   .   .   f. 1

The table is in another hand.

E. MSS.   4

2. Idem de cessatione legalium.
3. Idem de uenenis.

Collation: a¹² b⁸ c⁸ d¹² e¹⁴ (14 cancelled).

4. Questio prolixa disputata de differentia inter peccatum ueniale et mortale cum aliis tractatibus.

These 'alii tractatus' are numbered 24, 25, 26.

24. Ulterius restat.
25. Ex istis patescit.
26. Ulterius iuxta premissa.

Collation: a¹⁰ b¹⁰ (8–10 cancelled).

5. Expositio metologiarum (mytholog.) Fulgencii.

Inc. 'Intencio uenerabilis uiri fulgentii.' Imperfect at the end.

Collation: a¹⁰ (a leaf inserted between 9 and 10) b⁶ c¹² (wants 2: 1 is misbound, at the end).

Between pp. 122, 123 of the volume is a slip inserted with three diagrams, one of the arms of the Trinity, the other referring to *Bona temporalia.*

The book belonged to Kempston, and has his notice (see p. 8).

[C. M. A. 50.]

118. Bl. 3. 4.

BARTHOLOMAEI DE PISIS DE VITA S. FRANCISCI LIBRI III.

Vellum, 12¼ × 9¼, ff. 291, in double columns. Cent. xv. Written in Italy; in a fine hand.

Collation: 1 fly-leaf: a¹⁰–z¹⁰ aa¹⁰–ff¹⁰.

On f. 1 is a good miniature in the initial: S. Francis receives the stigmata, in a landscape coloured black and gold: Lib. II. has a good initial.

The work ends with the author's letter to the General of his order, and the answer of the latter.

On the fly-leaf is:

Iste liber competit loco sci Appolonii extra Brixiam.

No doubt given by Wotton.

[C. M. A. 59.]

119. Bl. 3. 5.

S. Gregorii Magni Epistolae, etc.

Vellum, 14⅛ × 9⅞, ff. 250, varying number of lines to a page. Cent. xiii. and xv. Binding: original, with beautiful stamps, of medallion and lozenge forms, representing (1) S. Barbara, crowned, with palm and tower, (2) S. Katherine, with sword and wheel, (3) a Paschal Lamb, (4) an Unicorn, (5) a Bat. The fly-leaves are from a gradual with music, and from a xvth cent. MS. (theological), in double columns.

Contents:

I. S. Gregorii Magni Epistolarum Libri xiv.

Preceded by a Table in triple columns, on four leaves. Cent. xiii. In double columns: the initials are good.

Collation: a⁴ i⁸–xii⁸ xiii⁶ xiv⁸–xxii⁸ xxiii⁶ (5, 6 cancelled): 182 leaves.

At the end is the entry of a *cautio*, or pledging of the book:

Exposita m. henrico swan xij die octob. anno dⁿⁱ mᵒ · cccc · lxvj pro · x · marcis, et habet secum Josephum in antiquitatibus, sanctum Thomam super 4 sententiarum, et augustinum de ciuitate dei.

II. 1. Vincentius Beluacensis de consolatione mortis . . f. 183

Cent. xv. Single lines, in a running hand.

    2. Idem de puerorum illustrium educatione 201
    3. Idem de uirtutibus antiquorum principum et philoso-
       phorum 235

Collation: a⁸–g⁸: 56 leaves.

III. 1. Crisostomus de reparatione lapsi 239

In double columns.

    2. Tabula 248

Collation: a⁸ b⁴: 12 leaves.

The volume was given by William Horman.

[C. M. A. 65.]

120. Bl. 3. 6.

SS. Augustini, Anselmi, etc., Tractatus varii.

Vellum, 13 × 9, ff. 356, in double columns of 68 lines each.
Cent. xiv. Well written, with fair initials.

Binding H.V.: chain-mark at bottom *R.* corner in front.

Collation: a¹²–d¹² e⁸ f¹² ‖ g¹²–i¹² ‖ k¹²–m¹² n⁶ ‖ o¹²–s¹² ‖ t¹²–z¹² aa¹² ‖
bb¹²–hh¹².

Contents :

I. S. Augustini Tractatus xxvi., viz.:

1. Dialectica.
2. Categoriae.
3. de mendacio.
4. de lxxxiii. quaestionibus.
5. de Poenitentia.
6. de Doctrina Christiana libb. iv.
7. de · x · plagis.
8. de Corruptione Legis et Gratiae.
9. de Laude caritatis.
10. unde malum ?
11. de Libero Voluntatis arbitrio libb. ii.
12. de Vera Innocentia.
13. de Opere monachorum.
14. de Singularitate Clericorum.
15. de Natura et Origine Animae libb. ii.
16. ad Dulcitium de viii. quaestionibus.
17. de Disciplina Christianorum.
18. de Agone Christiano.
19. de Assumptione B. Marie.
20. contra v. Haereses.
21. ad Inquisitiones Ianuarii libb. ii.
22. de Visitatione Infirmorum.
23. de Cognitione Verae Vitae.
24. de Gaudio electorum et supplicio damnatorum.
25. Retractationum libb. ii.
26. de Ecclesiasticis Dogmatibus.

II. S. Anselmi Tractatus xxiii., viz.:

1. Monologion.
2. Proslogion.
3. contra Insipientem.
4. de Veritate.
5. de Libertate Arbitrii.
6. de Casu diaboli.
7. de Incarnatione Verbi.
8. de Processione Spiritus Sancti.
9. Meditationes.
10. Vita Anselmi.
11. Epistola ad Guillelmum Abbatem Fiscanensem.
12. Disputatio inter Christianum et gentilem.
13. de Conceptione B. V. Mariae.
14. ad Innocentium Papam de Fulconio.
15. ad Canones Higden. et Lugdun.
16. de Sacrificio Azymi.
17. Similitudines.
18. Cur Deus Homo ?
19. de Grammatica.
20. de Concordia Praedestinationis et Praescientiae.
21. de Altercatione inter Augustinum et Pelagium.
22. de Lamentatione Anselmi.
23. de Virginali conceptu.

III. Boethii Tractatus iv., viz.:

1. de Sancta Trinitate.
2. de Professione Fidei Catholicae.
3. de Duabus Naturis et Una Persona in Christo.
4. de Unitate et Uno.

IV.   Hugo de S. Victore de Archa Noe.

V.   Quidam Sermones.

VI.   S. Joh. Chrysostomus de proditione Judae.

VII.   S. Joh. Damasceni Logica.

VIII.   „   „   Elementarium.

IX.   „   „   de duabus Voluntatibus.

X.   S. Dionysii Areopagitae Angelica Hierarchia.

XI.   „   „   Ecclesiastica Hierarchia.

XII.   „   „   de Diuinis Nominibus.

XIII.   „   „   Mystica Theologia.

XIV.   „   „   Epistola ad Gaium Monachum.

XV.   S. Bernardi Tractatus vi., viz.:

1.   de Gratia et Libero Arbitrio.
2.   de xii. gradibus Humilitatis.
3.   ad Cluniacenses Monachos.

4.   Sermo in illud *Missus est Gabriel.*
5.   Sermo in illud *Dixit Simon Petrus ad Jesum.*
6.   De Diligendo Deo.

XVI.   Quaedam allegoriae super aliquos libros bibliae.

XVII.   Sententiae Damasceni per iv. libros Sententiarum.

At the beginning is an inscription, carefully erased, beginning:

Liber fratris...... (six lines erased: then in line 7) anno gratie mᵒ. cccᵒ. octauo decimo.

Also an entry of cent. xv.:

Donum Johannis Borowe quondam socii huius regalis collegii.

[C. M. A. 14, 15, 24, 25, 29.]

121.   Bl. 3. 7.

CODEX CANONUM, GRAECE.

Paper, 14 × 9¼, pp. 1327, written in various hands.   Cent. xvii. There are slips of a MS. written in Italy in the binding. *Collation:* a⁸–pppp⁸.

Contents:

Praefatio Theodori Balsamonis . . . . p.   1
Nomocanon Photii, cum Comment. Balsamonis   3
Quaestiones quorundam Monachorum et responsa, cum commento
Theod. Balsamonis   202

Canones Apostolorum 210
       Nicaeni 272
       CPolitani 303
       Ephesini 320
       Chalcedonenses, cum Comment. Balsamonis . . . 333
de v^to Synodo 364
de vi^to Synodo 365
Praef. in Conciliorum Trullanum ; Canones Trullani . . . 365
Canones 2^di Nicaeni 504
Epistola Tarasii 570
Canones Synodi in Ecclesia Apostolorum 579
       in Eccl. S. Sophiae 613
Synodus Carthaginensis sub Cypriano 618
Canones Ancyrani 623
       Neocaesareenses, Gangrenses, Antiocheni, Laodiceni,
       Sardicenses.
       Diversorum conciliorum ; Carthaginenses . . . 773
Epist. Canonica Dionysii Alex. 1016
Canones Petri Alexandrini 1027
Epist. Canonica Gregorii Neocaesareensis 1050
       Athanasii ad Rufinianum 1079

Epist. Basilii ad Amphilochium (p. 1083), ad Diodorum Tarsen-
sem (1216), ad Gregorium presbyterum (1224), ad Chorepiscopos
(1231), ad Episcopos sibi subditos (1233), ejusdem de spiritu
sancto (1236 and 1244).

Epist. Canonica Gregorii Nysseni (1247). Responsa Timothei
Alex. (1285). Προσφώνησις Theophili Alex. (1296), ejusdem
ἀφήγησις de Catharis (1305). Ep. Canonica Cyrilli (1308).
Gregorii Naz. versus de Canone Scripturae (1317). Amphi-
lochii versus (1319). Gennadii CPolitani epist. encyclica (1321).
Basilii ex Epistola ad Nicopolitanos (1326). Fere omnia cum
commentario.

[C. M. A. 37, 38.]

122. Bl. 3. 8.

ARISTOTELIS ETHICA NICOMACHEA CUM COMMENTARIO EUSTATHII.

Vellum, $13\frac{1}{4} \times 9$, ff. 223, in double columns of 50 lines each.
Cent. xiv. In a hand resembling an Italian hand: good initials.

The text of Aristotle is underlined in red. Binding H.V. :
chain-mark at bottom R. front.

Collation : a^{12}–f^{12} g^{12} (wants three leaves) h^{12}–s^{12} t^{10}.

The volume is so tightly bound that I am unable to ascertain the exact structure of
quire g.

At the bottom of f. 1 *a* is :

Contenta : Textus Eticorum Aristotelis cum commento Eustracii.

The text begins :

Eustracii metropolitani Nikee enarracio in primum Aristotelis moralium ad Nico-machum.

Philosophia in duas partes diuisa.

Quire *h* begins :

Enarracio Ephesii domini Michaelis in quintum Moralium. In presenti v^{to} libro existente de negotio moralium.

The book was

Liber Will. Horman.

[C. M. A. 56.]

123. Bl. 3. 9.

MATTHAEI WESTMONASTERIENSIS FLORES HISTORIARUM.

Vellum, $10\frac{3}{4} \times 7\frac{3}{4}$, ff. 277, in double columns of 37 lines each. Cent. xiii. and xiv. In a fine hand.

Collation : a^{12} b^{14} c^{12} d^{14} e^{12} (misbound) $f^{12}-n^{12}$ o^{10} (10 cancelled) p^{10} q^{12} r^{12} s^{12} t^{12} u^{12} v^{12} x^{12} y^{10} $z^?$ (1–4 remain).

For a full account of the importance of this MS. see Dr Luard's edition of the Flores Historiarum in the Rolls Series (Vol. I. p. xv).

It was written at the Priory of Merton, in Surrey. The hand changes after the year 1294.

The MS. is imperfect, ending in the year 1306, with the words:

Circa festum Cathedre S. petri venit quidam Cardi.....

There are a few pictures, viz.:

1. f. 27 *b*. The Nativity : the Virgin in bed (asleep) : star above : over it, the Child, ox, and ass. Joseph on *R*. : gold ground.

2–10. Coronations of Kings from William I. (f. 158) to Edward I.: these are all very much alike, each representing a seated King between two Bishops (or Archbishops), who are crowning him.

On f. 1 *a* is the word Liber... : the rest being totally erased. The book formerly belonged to Archbishop Parker.

[C. M. A. 58.]

124. Bl. 3. 10.

JOHANNIS DIACONI VITAE S. GREGORII LIBRI IV.

Vellum, 12⅝ × 8, ff. 137, 30 lines to a page. Cent. xi. Written in Italy.

Collation : a⁸–f⁸ g⁶ h⁸–r⁸ s⁴ (4 cancelled): 3 fly-leaves.

There are fine interlaced initials and *capitula* to each book. On f. 122 *a* is a most interesting outline drawing of the Funeral of S. Gregory. The façade of the old Basilica of S. Peter's is very accurately represented, with the bronze peacocks on the outer corners, and the original mosaics, of the Lamb, the Four Beasts, and the Twenty-four Elders[1].

The text of the Life of S. Gregory is followed by:

2. Gregorius Leudelrade regi Langobardorum, on the last leaf,

and

3. (in a later hand) Epistola Bernardi Clareuall. karissimo suo fratri et domino Ad. dei gratia F. (? Farfensi) abbati.

The fly-leaves, which are cut and mutilated, contain letters of Popes Anastasius, Eugenius, and the Emperor Frederic, relating to the monastery of Farfa, to which the MS. must have belonged.

One, at the end, from Eugenius, is dated from Florence in 1440.

On the margins of ff. 3 *b*, 4 *a*, are letters of cent. xiii. from Hugh, Bishop of Ostia and Velletri, to the Abbot of Farfa, and from a Provost and Prior of S. Salvator to Hugh.

The name Jo. Delphini is on the second fly-leaf at the beginning.

The MS. no doubt came from Wotton.

[C. M. A. 70.]

125. Bl. 3. 11.

HISTORIA SCHOLASTICA PETRI MANDUCATORIS.

Vellum, 12¼ × 9, ff. 171, in double columns of 50 lines each. Cent. xiii. (early). French hand, in quires of 8 leaves.

---

[1] I had this drawing photographed, and copies have been sent to Cav. De Rossi, Sig. Lanciani, and M. Rohault de Fleury. Professor Grisar is about to reproduce it in the *Römische Quartalschrift für Archäologie.*

The text is followed by the Epitaph of the author, as usual.

There is a fine initial at the beginning: also many marginal notes. Three leaves at the beginning, and seven pages at the end, are covered with miscellaneous notes and verses. Among them the *Liber Methodii* (often printed, e.g. in the *Orthodoxographa* of J. Grynaeus), a list of the Ten Plagues, a definition of history, the Hebrew alphabet, genealogies, and the Apostles' Creed.

[C. M. A. 41.]

126. Bl. 3. 12.

IOANNIS FILII SERAPIONIS MEDICA QUAEDAM.

Vellum, 13½ × 9½, ff. 118 + 2 blank, in double columns of 52 lines each. Cent. xv. In quires of 8 leaves, except the first, which is of 4 (the 4th cancelled).

Contents:

1.	Index (perhaps written by Darell, see p. 27) . . . . f.		i
2.	Abbreuiatum Ioannis de causis et signis egritudinis: tractatus septem, viz.:		
	a. de egritudinibus capitis		1
	b. ,, oculorum, etc.		12
	c. ,, stomachi, etc.		25
	d. ,, aepatis, etc.		35
	e. ,, in cute, etc.		53
	f. de febribus		68
	g. antidotarius		74
3.	Eiusdem synonima		116

The MS. belonged to W. Horman.

[C. M. A. 84.]

127. Bl. 3. 13.

MEDICA QUAEDAM.

Vellum, 13½ × 9¾, ff. 275 + 6 fly-leaves. Text surrounded by comment. Cent. xiv. The hand resembles an Italian hand. The initials are good: there are many notes on the fly-leaves.

Contents :

1.   Isagoge Joannicii, preceded by a Table on f. 1   .   .   . f.   4
2.   Philaretus de pulsibus   .   .   .   .   10 *b*
3.   Theophilus de urinis   .   .   .   .   12 *b*
4.   Aphorismi Hippocratis cum commento Galieni   .   .   .   22
5.   Prognostica Hippocratis cum commento Galieni   .   .   .   87
6.   Regimen Hippocratis cum commento Galieni   133
7.   Tegni siue ars parua Galieni cum commento Hali   .   .   .   183
     Galieni opera recensentur   .   .   .   .   271 *b*

This last item forms part of no. 7.

Colophon :

> Explicit commentum hali super tegni galieni.
> Hostia que deus es que cunctis sola salus es
> Salues infirmos serues ad premia firmos.

On the last fly-leaf are many *Cautiones.*   One is dated 1342, the next is :

> Caucio mag. Joh. Sukelyn exposita in Cista Wynton.......proxima post festum trans.
> S. Thome a. d. Mᵘ. cccᵒ. liᵒ.

A third in Cista Wynton. is dated 1391.
On f. 1 is :

> Donum Gulielmi Horman.

[C. M. A. 97.]

128.   Bl. 4. 1.

LEONIS BAPTISTAE ALBERTI DE RE AEDIFICATORIA LIBRI X.

Paper, 13 × 8¼, ff. 244, 30 lines to a page.   Cent xv.   Written in Italy, in a fine cursive hand.   In quires of 10 leaves.

Binding of red leather, stamped with border of cable-pattern, probably Venetian.

On f. 1 *a* is a fine initial in gold and colours.

On the lower margin is a shield (that of B. Bembo, the owner), *azure*, a chevron *or* between three four-petalled flowers of the second : the shield is between branches of palm and bay.

Each of the ten books has a good initial.   After f. 221 are six blank leaves of paper and one of parchment.   These are followed by a tract on six leaves in another hand, beginning abruptly :

> ' Primus arius radix unitas diuinitati consecratus est.'

It relates to lines and architecture.

The MS. belonged to Bernardo Bembo. On f. 208 is a long marginal note by him, as follows (the text alludes to Nemi):

Vidimus Nemorensem locum et lacum et lucum amoenissimum atque pomiferum hortum omnibus deliciis refertissimum Aquis perfossum montem egredientibus ut perennes nihil redundent iisdem alligate limitibus Celum et agros elysios facile dixeris, illum ad omnes ueneres hylarem. Eius profectionis in causa fuit Rev^{mus} Joh. Card. Columna, Vir apprime solide illius uirtutis ex qua Virum credimus Sane totius humanitatis exemplar. Qui tametsi magnitudinem animi et non fucate nobilitatis symulacrum est, identidem ueterem etiam Romanam illam ac ueram propaginem representat ut nihil degenerasse prioris succis aurea illa poma credideris. Redeo ad causam profectionis. Fuerat ergo restituendi imperii et possessionis Nemoralis eiusdem arretie Rev^{mo} quem prefati sumus Cuius · x · integros annos expers manserat, Xistique pontificis optione et rogatu quem abrogauimus ipsi, una collega et oratore clar^{mo} equite Sebastiano Baduario indulctis ad hoc facientibus Jnnocentii · viii · Pontificis cuius fides egregia eius rei arbitrium nobis demandauit. Anno Sal. lxxxviiij super M. cccc^{tos} Johanne Vrtica et Petro filio comitibus jucundissimis. Hec Bernardi Bembi manus.

The MS. was doubtless given by Wotton.

[C. M. A. 4.]

129. Bl. 4. 2.

ARISTOTELIS ETHICA, ETC.

Vellum, 10⅝ × 7½, ff. 217, 33 lines to a page. Cent. xiii., xiv. Binding H.V.

Contents:

  1. Aristotelis Ethicorum libri x. Cent. xiii. . . . . f. 1

In a pointed hand with flourished initials.
Collation: a⁶ b⁸ c⁸, etc., ff. 66.

  2. Aristotelis Polyticorum libri viii. Cent. xiv. . . . . f. 67

In an Italian hand. The initial has a picture of Aristotle, half-length, with book, clad in red and pink.
Collation: a¹⁰–h¹⁰ i⁸ (8 cancelled), ff. 87.

  3. Tractatus de Bona Fortuna, ff. 3 ⎱ in the same hand as 2.
  4. de ebdomadibus Boetii, ff. 2 ⎰
  5. Aristotelis Retoricorum libri iii. Cent. xiv.

In another Italian hand. The first initial has two half-length figures of men teaching: one holds a book, the other a roll. In the border is a bearded man, half-length, and an angel with trumpet.   In the initial to Book iii. a half-length man with a book, speaking.

6. Aristotelis Poetica.   In the same hand.

Colophon :

Primus Aristotelis de arte poetica liber explicit Alleluia.

Collation : a¹²–e¹² f ⁴, ff. 64.

[C. M. A. 13.]

130. Bl. 4. 3.

Disputatio Petri Prioris, etc.

Vellum, 12½ × 8⅜, ff. 306.   Two volumes in one.   Cent. xiii. and xiv.

Contents :

1. Disputatio Petri Prioris SS. Trinitatis Londini contra Iudaeos ad Stephanum Archiepiscopum Cantuariensem et Cardinalem.   Cent. xiv.

In 3 books : in quires of 12 leaves, the last of 8, the last 4 blank : ff. 236.   In double columns of 70 lines each.

Leland (*De Script. Brit.*) and Bale (*Cent.* III. 90) call this writer Petrus Canonicus, and say that the book was dedicated to Simon Langton, younger brother of Stephen, and Archdeacon of Kent.   The author's date is given as 1230.

2. S. Thomas super Dionysium de diuinis nominibus.   Cent. xiii., xiv.

In another hand ; in double columns of 51 lines each.

Collation : a¹²–e¹² f ¹⁰, ff. 70.

[C. M. A. 55.]

131. Bl. 4. 4.

Cassiodorii Historia Tripartita, etc.

Vellum, 12 × 8, ff. 225, in double columns of 49 lines each. Cent. xiv., xv.

Collation : i¹²–xi¹² xii¹² (11, 12 canc.) xiii¹²–xvi¹² xvii¹² (11, 12 canc.) ‖ a⁸ b⁶ (6 canc.).

Contents :

1. Magni Aur. Cassiodorii Historia Tripartita . . . . f. 1

There is a border to f. 1.

2. Martini Gemblacensis de ordine predicatorum Chronicon . 142

The text extends to 1285 : two leaves follow, with Tables of Emperors and Popes.

Three blank leaves.

3. Vegetius de re militari 190

In another hand : in double columns.

The book has on the fly-leaf :

Donum M. Rogeri Lupton Juris canonici professoris et huius collegii quondam prepositi.

[C. M. A. 36.]

132. Bl. 4. 5.

GALENI QUAEDAM.

Vellum, $10\frac{1}{2} \times 7\frac{3}{8}$, ff. 282, double columns of 51 lines. Cent. xiii. Binding H.V. In quires of 12 and 8 leaves. Table on f. 1 b.

In hoc volumine continentur libri infrascripti.

1. Primus l. de criticis diebus.
2. Item de crisi.
3. de morbo et accidente.
4. de interioribus.
5. megategni.
6. de ingenio sanitatis.
7. de tactu pulsus.
8. de voce et anelitu.
9. de anathomia.
10. de secretis.
11. de spermate uel de xii. portis.
12. de simplici medicina.
13. de malicia complexionis diuerse.
14. de iuuamentis membrorum.
15. de elementis.
16. de complexionibus.

The initials to the books are of very good xiiith cent. style.

Between nos. 11 and 12 are two pages of *sortes*, with accompanying diagrams, neatly written, probably of cent. xiii., xiv. They may be worth transcribing.

The diagrams are mainly wheels of 12 divisions, each headed with the name of a region. Below, the oracles appertaining to each are given. The names of countries seem derived from an oriental source: Babilonia, Elzeuge, Francia, Elmutecima, Elbulgor, Eltafiac, Farisei, Romania.

The last two pages of the book are covered with prayers composed of magical names, connected with the *Ars notoria*.

[C. M. A. 46.]

133. Bl. 4. 6 [olim Bo. 6. 1].

OROSII HISTORIA.

Vellum, 11 × 7¾, ff. 87, in double columns of 39 lines each. Cent. xiii. (early). In a fine hand with plain initials, generally red or green.

Binding original: white skin over boards: formerly clasped, strap and pin fastening: chain-mark apparently on lower edge of front cover. On the back is the name OROSIUS in Lombardic capitals of cent. xiii.–xiv. This is often found on MSS. belonging to Bury Abbey.

Provenance. On f. 1 is the name *W. Bathon.* The MS. must have belonged to Laud when Bishop of Bath and Wells.

On a paper fly-leaf is:

Dedit hunc librum Collegio Etonensi Thomas Richardson S. T. P. eiusdem Collegij Socius 1722.

Collation: a⁸–f⁸ g⁸ (wants 2) h⁸ (wants 8) i⁸ k⁸ (2 cancelled or replaced) l⁸ (wants 1) m⁸ (wants 3–8): quires numbered i–xi on last leaf: catchwords later: 87 leaves.

On ff. 15 *b*, 16, occurs some very odd *spaced* writing, in shorter lines than usual, and written dispersedly, as if too much space had been allowed for the matter, and another quire already begun.

Contents:

1. Orosii Historia . . . . f. 1 *a*

The initial to Book i. is cut out: the first leaves have suffered from damp.

2.   Epistola Alexandri ad Aristotelem .   .   .   .   .   . f. 85 *a*
     Inc. Semper memor fui.

Ends imperfectly :

Detractisque cornibus et dentibus insigni onustus preda in castra......

[C. M. A. *vac.*]

134.   Bl. 4. 7.

ROBERTI CRIKELADENSIS PRIORIS OXONIENSIS EXCERPTA
EX PLINII HISTORIA NATURALI.

Vellum, 11⅝ × 8, ff. 164, in double columns of 29 lines each.
Cent. xii., xiii. In a large English hand. There is a good initial
to the first Book.

In quires of 8 leaves, the last of 4 ; 3 blank fly leaves.

The extracts extend from Book ii.–ix. of the History, and are
headed by an extract from Tranquillus (= Suetonius), 'in catalogo
uirorum illustrium de Plinio.'

Leland (p. 234) calls this writer Robertus Cornutus, and assigns
his date to the reigns of Richard I. and John.

[C. M. A. 57.]

135.   Bl. 4. 8.

L. ANNAEI SENECAE EPISTOLAE.

Vellum, 11⅝ × 7¾, ff. 167, 26 lines to a page. Cent. xii. The
writing is large, probably Italian.

Collation : a² (1 cancelled) i⁸–xx⁸ xxi⁸ (8 cancelled).

The title page (f. 1 *b*) is framed in black, with interesting ornaments : the title is written in red and green :

In hoc volumine continentur Epistole Senece ad Lucilium numero octoginta novem.

Prefixed are :

(*a*)   A notice from Hieronymus in Catalogo virorum illustrium.
(*b*)   Epistolae Senecae et Pauli.
(*c*)   Epitaphium Senecae.

On the last leaf, in a smaller hand, are :

Versus de rerum mutabilitate.
Nuper eram locuplex, etc.

On the fly-leaves are notes in an Italian hand of cent. xv., probably Bernardo Bembo's; one is dated 1488. xxii *Octobris Ro(mae) opitulante altissimo.* Another relates to Dante's arms, which are sketched, and the tinctures written on the shield: party per pale *rosso* and *azzurro* a fess *biancho.*

Wafered into the book is the following letter :

Marce, heri in uisitatione Reverendissimi domini Cardinalis Legati fui inuitatus ab eo ut hodie secum accedam ad sanctum Nicolaum de littore ubi est diem hunc acturus. accedam igitur. si forte necesse fuerit expedire litteras Imperatoris cape eas a dominico nostro Bellono et signa atque domino Alexandro da. Item litteras regis Francorum habes tu. Ducis Burgundie habet ille adolescens Bartholomeus. regis Boemie habet Sebastianus. Si ita opus sit, etiam ipsas signa et expedi, ne uideamur forte nostra munia neglexisse. Vale. xxiij Augusti 1463 venetie

Nicol. Sagundinus pater tuus.

The MS. must have come from Wotton.

[C. M. A. 112.]

136. Bl. 4. 9.

L. Annaei Senecae Epistolae Italice.

Vellum, 12¼ × 9, ff. 124, in double columns of 45 lines each. Cent. xv.

Written in Italy. There are beautiful borders to the Table of Contents and to the first page of the text. In the initial of the former is a head.

Collation: a⁸–o⁸ p¹².

The Epistles are followed by :

(*a*) Jerome's notice of Seneca.
(*b*) The Letters of Paul and Seneca.

Colophon :

Scritto per me lorenzo di stefano sambarducci pplo (? preso) san filicie impiazza : deo gratia.

Doubtless given by Wotton.

[C. M. A. 111.]

137. Bl. 4. 10.

Vitruvii de Architectura Libri x.

Vellum, $12\frac{1}{4} \times 8\frac{1}{8}$, ff. 64, 51 lines to a page. Cent. xiv., xv. Written in Italy.

The initial to Book i. has a half-length figure of Vitruvius, in cap, holding an adze and a hatchet.

That to Book ii. has a half-length of Hercules, bearded, holding club and lion's skin.

Collation: a¹⁰ b⁸ c¹⁰–f¹⁰ g⁸ (5, 6 cancelled, 7, 8 blank).

On the fly-leaves are the following notes:

(1) Ludouici Rigii Cornarii. Obiit dignus uir x° Octobris 1492. N. 76. Vetruvio de architetura.

(2) Codex patricii Veneti (erasure: probably *Bernardi Bembi*) olim D. Jac. Lingusci.

(3) Vetruuius Nobilis Archytectus exactissimi uir ingenii. Olim ex biblioteca clarissimi Mathematici Jacobi Langusci Veneti. Post eius casum patauij sub astatione multis cum aliis in nostratium cytum¹ deductus est. Anno saluatoris M. cccc. liii°. Tandem multiplici amicorum indulctu prebito quod raritas tunc librorum effecerat, Veluti transfuga ·xx· ferme annos nobis delituit nescio ne obscurus in ulua ut poeta diceret. Demum hodie Paulus Cornelius Ludouici filius quem de Arrigio dictitant, id certior factus ex nostratibus hunc fuisse nobilem Archytectum, bonam mentem indutus Veteri domino destinandum curauit. Quod bono omine xvi Junij 1493 factum est. Quo die opportune sermo est diuinus in missarum solenniis quanti habenda sit deperditorum recuperatio, et quod celebri gaudio exilarandum sit mentibus Angelorum cum redemptio est deperditarum animarum insperato facta, his qui iacturam optatissimarum quidem et usu suauissimarum magni pensandum esse statuerunt. Juxta illud petrarce uersum: che piu gloria è nel regno degli ellecti Dun spirito converso et piu si stima Che de nouanta noue altri perfecti.

Idibus Nouembribus Bernardi Bembi doctoris manus.

No doubt from Wotton.

[C. M. A. 125.]

138. Bl. 4. 11.

Iuvenalis et Persii Satirae: codex impressus.

Paper, $11 \times 7\frac{1}{4}$. Printed at Milan by Phil. Lauanius, 1476.

The initials are finely painted, and there are many marginal notes in a most exquisite small Italian hand.

The fly-leaves are from a Missal of cent. xiv. On one at the beginning is a note, in Bernardo Bembo's hand, as I think:

¹ ? *cyclum* in the sense of 'book-case.'

Inceptus die...Marcij 1481, incepi cum domino episcopo Bellunensi domino Bernardo
Rubeo die 26 Decembris 1486, cuius magister domus eram.

Rev^{mus} In Christo pater Dominus Episcopus Belunensis Dominus Bernardus Rubeus
assumpsit Rotum in Ciuitate Venetia in S. Georgio maiore die undecima mensis Septem-
bris 1487 hora : 19 :

Another erased note follows.

On the last fly-leaf was a long note, now erased, which ends :

ex pleni con supra scripto D. Ber. Rubeo Episc. Bellunensi die 16 Octobr. 1489.

The name Jo. Delphini is on the lower margin of f. 1.

The book was no doubt given by Wotton.

[C. M. A. 87.]

139. Bl. 4. 12.

HOMERI ILIADIS LIBRI V. GRAECE.

Vellum, 12 × 8¾, ff. 76, text surrounded by scholia.   Cent. xiii. (?)
In a very fine hand: the title is in gold.   The MS. is much stained
in parts.

Collation: a⁸–θ⁸ ι⁸ (5–8 cancelled).

The text ends with v. 84 :

ὣς οἱ μὲν πονέοντο κατὰ κρατερὴν ὑσμίνην.

No doubt from Wotton.

[C. M. A. 78.]

140. Bl. 4. 13.

CL. PTOLEMAEI COSMOGRAPHIA LATINE.

Vellum, 11⅛ × 8⅛, ff. 138, 38 lines to a page.   Cent. xv.   Written
in Italy, in a beautiful hand.

Collation: a¹⁰ b¹⁰ c⁸ d¹⁰–g¹⁰ h⁸ i¹⁰–n¹⁰ o¹⁰ (+ a sheet inserted between
9 and 10).

Fol. 1 has a miniature in a gold frame extending across the
page.   On the *L.* a crowned and turbaned king sits, facing *R.*, on
a throne of metal.   He bends forward to receive a green book from
Ptolemy, who, in purple, bearded and hooded, kneels, holding in

his *L.* hand a circular planisphere on a stand: the face of it is divided into six equal parts by three diameters: two of these parts, on *L.*, contain the numbers 7 and 14; the two opposite divisions inscribed 6 and 9: on *R.* are three men, turbaned, and a camel: a landscape behind. The page is bordered: in the lower margin two genii hold a bay wreath enclosing a wheel party per fess *gules* and *argent*, counterchanged.

Each of the eight books has a good initial and partial border.
The colophon is simply LAVS DEO.
Doubtless given by Wotton.

[C. M. A. 107.]

141. Bl. 4. 14.

STRABONIS GEOGRAPHICORUM LIBRI X. GRAECE.

Paper, $11\frac{1}{2} \times 8$, ff. 300, 28 lines to a page. Cent. xv. (1430?). Binding, calf of cent. xviii. No doubt given by Sir Henry Wotton.

Collation: a^{10} (wants 1 blank) $\beta^{10}-\eta^{10}$ θ^4 ι^{10} ιa^{10} $\iota\beta^{10}$ $\iota\gamma^8$ $\iota\delta^{6(+6*)}$ $\iota\epsilon^{10}$ $\iota\varsigma^{14}$ $\iota\zeta^{10}$ $\iota\eta^{10}$ $\iota\theta^{10}$ κ^{10} κa^{12+2} (κa has two leaves inserted between 10 and 12 [end of Book vii.]) $\kappa\beta^{10}-\kappa\varsigma^{10}$ $\kappa\zeta^{10}$ (9 cancelled) $\kappa\eta^3$ $\kappa\theta^{10}$ λ^{10} λa^{10} (2 cancelled); 300 leaves.

The quires are marked on upper *R.* corner of first leaf, and lower margin of last leaf.

Contents:

Capitula, with a good ornament, and ΑΓΑΘΗΙ ΤΥΧΗΙ at the top of f. 1.
Book i. Headed in capitals, ΑΓΑΘΗΙ ΤΥΧΗΙ ΣΤΡΑΒΩΝΟΣ ΓΕΩΓΡΑΦΙΚΩΝ ·Ā· . . . . f. 3

The first page in a larger hand, only 10 lines.

Book ii. . . . . 43 *b*
Book iii. ὑποκείσθω δὴ σφαιροειδὴς ἡ γῆ (II. v. p. 177 Tauchnitz). 72

The hand changes after f. 81 for two leaves, of which the first has 39 lines to the page, the second 29 and 22 lines, on the recto and verso.

The writing is by the original scribe, and the marginal notes do not differ from those elsewhere in the book.

f. 81 ends :

εἰσπλέουσι τοίνυν τὸν κατὰ στήλας πορθμὸν ἐν δεξιᾷ μέν ἐστιν ἡ λιβύη (p. 201).

At the bottom, in red :

✠ ἔλιπεν ἀπὸ τοῦ πρωτοτύπου τέτραδιν· καὶ ὁ εὑρήσων ἀναπληρωσάτω.

The two supply-leaves contain the beginning of Book iii. (without title), ἀποδεδωκόσι δ᾽ ἡμῖν (p. 218, ed. Tauch.), to the words Ἀνάγκη δὲ διὰ πλειόνων (p. 223).

Book iv. 108

On f. 109 b, 110 a, the hand enlarges, as on the supply-leaves above. So on 112 b, 113, 116, 117 a. On f. 112 b is the note ἔλιπεν ἐκ τοῦ πρωτοτύπου φύλλα δύο.

After 122 a leaf is cancelled.

Book v. 130

On 142 b is the note in red : ἐνταῦθα λείπει τέτραδον ἕν, which apparently refers to the words following, ᾤκουν καθ᾽ αὑτοὺς (i. p. 372). However they, and the next 8 leaves, are supplied in the sloping hand, probably by the same scribe. The supply extends to ἤδη δὲ καὶ ὁ Σουρεντῖνος (p. 323).

Book vi. . . . . 156 b
Book vii. . . . . 179 b

ff. 202 b–205 a are in the larger sloping hand. At the top of 202 b is λείπει φύλλον ἕν. The passage supplied is Μετὰ δὲ Ὀγχησμὸν (ii. p. 119) to Κινέας δὲ μυθωδέστερον (the fragmentary end of the viith book, p. 127).

Book viii. . . . . 205 b

On f. 225 a spaces are left, shewing a mutilation in four lines in the archetype. So on 227 a (two lines).

Book ix. 240

A mutilation in six (or seven) lines is indicated on 240 a, and in four lines on 246 a : also on 249 b, 250 b, 251 a, 253, 256, 258, 281 : after 263 a leaf is cancelled.

Book x. 273

After 293 a leaf is cancelled.

Ends on 300 *a* :

Rubr. τέλος τοῦ Ιου καὶ τῆς Εὐρώπης περιοδείας.

Green. Ἐκτησάμην τήνδε τὴν βίβλον ἐκ Βυζαντίου γραφεῖσαν παρὰ Ἀγαλλιανοῦ διακόνου ἱερομνήμονος φίλου.

The verso is blank.

At the beginning is a parchment leaf, with a note of cent. xvii.:

Strabo. Continentur in hoc volumine x tantummodo libri.

There are many marginal notes in pink, blue, green, yellow, purple and black ink. Many of those in pink are by the original scribe Agallianos. Those in blue, green, purple and yellow are mostly by·(or from) Cyriacus of Ancona: others in pink, green and black are in a later and more pointed hand.

The contents of these scholia are, as far as I have examined them, not important, save a few of those written by Cyriacus. Of these I append all that relate to inscriptions: some have been rather inaccurately printed in the Oxford Strabo (1807).

1.   f. 149 *b*. (ιϛ : f. 10 *b*), on Book V. iv. p. 390, Tauch.

On Ancona : (C. I. L. IX. 5894).

ὡς δὲ ἄλλοι φασὶν ἦν πρὸς τῇ πόλει ταύτῃ τῆς ἀφροδίτης ἱερόν· διὸ καὶ ὁ Ἰουουενάλης εἷς τῶν λατίνων σατύρων ποιητὴς φησίν.

Ante domum Veneris qua*m* dorica substinet Ancon.

In the lower margin :

ἐστὶ δὲ ἐν τῇ στοᾷ ἐπὶ τοῦ λιμένος εἰς τὴν αὐτὴν πόλιν ἀνκῶνα πρὸς τὸν αὐξήσαντα τραϊανὸν ἐπίγραμμα τόδε.

IMP · CAESARI · DIVI · NERVAE · F · NERVAE · TRAIANO · OPTIMO · AVG · GERMANIC ·		
	DACICO · PONT · MAX · TR · POT · XVIII · IMP · IXI ·	
	COS · VI · PP · PROVIDENTISSIMO · PRINCIPI · ℰ	DIVAE
PLOTINAE	SENATVS · P · Q · R · QVOD ACCESSVM · ITALIAE ·	MARCIANAE
AVG ·	HOC · ETIAM · ADDITO EX PECVNIA · SVA · PORTV ·	AVG ·
CONIVGI AVG ·	TVTIOREM · NAVIGANTIBVS · REDDIDERIT · ℰ	SORORI · AVG ·

2.   f. 222 *b* (κγ : f. 7 *b*), Book VIII. iv. (ii. 180 Tauch.).

On Methone : (C. I. G. 1323).

Τόδ' ἐγὼ κυριακὸς εἰς μεσσηνιακὸν πύλον ἐπίγραμμα εὖρον.

ΑΥΤΟΚΡΑΤΟΡΑ · ΚΑΙϹΑΡΑ | ΜΑΡΚΟΝ · ΑΝΤѠΝΙΟΝ𝒴 | ΓΟΡΔΙΑ-
ΝΟΝ ΕΥϹΕΒΗ | ΕΥΤΥΧΗ · ϹΕΒΑϹΤΟΝ |
ΗΠΟΛΙϹ · ΗΒΕΙΤΥΛΕѠΝ | ΔΙΕΦΟΡѠΝ · ΤѠΝΠΕΡΙ | ΜΑΡΚΟΝ ·
ΑΥΡΗΛΙΟΝ | ΝΕΙΚΗΦΟΡΟΝ · ΠΡΟϹΔΕ|ΚΤΟΥ.

καὶ νυνὶ δὲ ταύτην ἐλαττωμένην πυλων πόλιν βελτῦλον καλοῦσιν.

3. f. 223 *a* (*κγ*: f. 8 *a*), VIII. iv. (l. c. p. 182). (C. I. G. 1297.)

ἐγὼ δὲ κυριακὸς εἰς ἰθώμην μεσσηνίων ἀκρόπολιν τόδ' ἐπίγραμμα εἰς λίθον εὗρον.

ΕΠΙ · ΙΕΡΕΟΣ · ΚΡΕΣ|ΦΟΝΙΟΥ · ΕΤΟΥΣ · | ΡΝΖ | ΑΓΩΝΟΘΕΤΗΣ |
ΤΙΒ · ΚΛΑΥΔΙΟΣ · ΚΡΙΣΠΙΑΝ|ΟΥ · ΥΙΟΣ · ΑΡΙΣΤΟΜΕΝΗΣ.

4. f. 224 *b* (*κγ*: f. 9 *b*), VIII. v. p. 186.

On Taenarum : (C. I. G. 1393).

Ḣ · ΠΟΛΙC|Ḣ · ΤΑΙΝΑΡΙѠΝ | ΤΙΒΕΡΙΟΝ ΚΛΑΥΔΙ|ΟΝ · ΧΑΡΤѠ-
ΝΑ|ΤΟΝ · ΑΡΙϹΤΟΝ ΠΟ|ΛΕΙΤΗΝ · ϹΟΦΡΟϹΥ|ΝΗϹΤΕΚΑΙ · ΤΗϹ · ΠΕ|
ΡΙΤΗΝ · ΑΓΟΡΑΝΟ|ΜΙΑΝ · ΑΝΥΠΕΒΛ|ΗΤΟΥ · ΦΙΛΟΤΕΙΜΙΑϹ | ΕΙΝΕ-
ΚΕΝ · | Ψ̄ Η. Β̄ ϱ.

sic

5. f. 226 *a* (*κδ*: f. 1 *a*), VIII. vi. p. 190. (C. I. G. 1389.)

On Eurycles :

καὶ ἡμεῖς εἰς ταινάριον περὶ αὐτοῦ υἱοῦ λάκωνος τόδε ἐπίγραμμα εὗρον (*sic*).

ΤΟ · ΚΟΙΝΟΝ · ΤѠΝ ΕΛΕΥΘΕ|ΡΟΛΑΚѠΝѠΝ · ΓΑΪΟΝ | ΙΟΥΛΙΟΝ ·
ΛΑΚѠΝΑ · ΕΥΡΥΚΛΕΟΥΣ · ΥΙΟΝ · | ΤΟΝ · ΙΔΙΟΝ · ΕΥΕΡΓΕΤΗΝφ |
ΔΑΜΑΡΜΕΝΙΔΑϹ | ΣΤΡΑΤΗΓѠΝ | ΕΠΕΜΕΛΗΘΗ ꝃ.

6. f. 230 *b* (*κδ*: 5 *b*), VIII. vi. p. 203.

On Kalaureia : (C. I. G. 1188).

Η · ΕΥΜΕΝΕΙΑ · | ΒΑΣΙΛΕΟΣ · ΑΤΤΑΛΟΥ · Α · ΠΟΛΙΣ|Α · ΤѠΝ ·
ΚΑΛΑΥΡΕΑΤΑΝ · ΑΝΕΘΗ | ΚΕΝ · ΑΡΕΤΑΣΕΝΕΚΕΝ · ΚΑΙ
ΕΥΕΡ|ΓΕΣΙΑΣ · ΤΑΣ · ΕΙΣ · ΤΕ ΘΕΟΝ · ΚΑΙ ΑΥ|ΤΑΝ · ΚΑΙ

sic

ΤΟΥΣ ΑΛΛ | ΟΥΣ ΕΑΛΛΑΝΑΣ.

7. f. 243 *b* (*κε* : 8 *b*), IX.

At Athens : (C. I. G. 478).

ἡμεῖς δὲ ἐν τῇ τῶν ἀθηναίων ἀκροπόλει ἐς τὸ τῆς πολιάδος ἀθηνᾶς ἱερὸν καὶ προπυλαίων
κατοφλίον τόδε εἰς λατίνων ὀνόματος τϊμὴν ὑπογραφὴν ἴδον.

Ο ΔΗΜΟΣ · ΘΕΑΙ · ΡѠΜΗΙ · ΚΑΙ ΣΕΒΑΣΤѠΙ ΚΑΙΣΑΡΙ · ΣΤΡΑ-
ΤΗΓΟΥΝΤΟΣ ·· ΕΠΙ · ΤΟΥΣ | ΟΠΛΙΤΑΣ · ΠΑΜΜΕΝΟΥΣ · ΤΟΥ · ΖΗ-
ΝѠΝΟΣ · ΜΑΡΑΘѠΝΙΟΥ · ΙΕΡΕѠΣ · ΘΕΑΣ · ΡѠΜΗΣ · ΚΑΙ | ΣΕΒΑ-
ΣΤΟΥ · ΣѠΤΗΡΟΣ · ΕΠΑΚΡΟΠΟΛΕΙ · ΕΠΙ ΙΕΡΕΙΑΣ · ΑΘΗΝΑΣ · ΠΟ-
ΛΙΑΔΟΣ· ΜΕΓΙΣΤΗΣ | ΤΗΣ · ΑΣΚΛΗΠΙΔΟΥ · ΑΛΑΙΕѠΣ · ΘΥΓΑΤΡΟΣ ·
ΕΠΙΑΡΧΟΝΤΟΣ · ΑΡΗΟΥ · ΤΟΥ · ΜѠΡΙѠΝΟΣ . ΠΑΙΑΝΙΕѠΣ ϱ.

8. f. 254 b (κϛ : f. 9 b), IX. ii. p. 269.

On Lebadea : (C. I. G. 1603).

ἡμεῖς δὲ ἐν Λεβαδίᾳ τόδε εἰς ὀρεινῆς κορυφὴν ἐπίγραμμα εὗρον, ἐν τῷ παλαιῷ δὲ ἐρειπίῳ
τε καὶ πανταχοῦ κεχαλασμένῳ ἱερῷ· ὃ νυνὶ ἅγιον ἡλίαν καλοῦσιν.

ΗΡΑ · ΒΑΣΙΛΙΔΙ · ΚΑΙ · ΤΗΙ · ΠΟΛΕΙ · ΤΩΝ · ΛΕΒΑΔΕΩΝ ·
ΜΕΝΑΝΔΡΟΣ · ΧΡΗΣΙΜΟΥ · ΙΕΡΙΤΕΥΣΑΣ · ΠΕΝΤΕΤΗΡΙΔΑ (ἐκ τῶν
ἰδίων ἀνέθηκεν) ΙΕΡΙΤΕΥΟΥΣΗΣ | ΓΥΝΑΙΚΟΣ ΑΥΤΟΥ · ΠΑΡΙΣΙΑΣ ·
ΤΗΣ · ΟΝΑΣΙΜΒΡΟΤΟΥ ϙ.

9. f. 258 b (κζ : f. 3 b), IX. p. 280.

On Delphi : (C. I. G. 1644).

ἡμεῖς δὲ ἐν Δελφοῖς παραγενόμενοι, εἰς ἐρειπίαν τοῦ ἱεροῦ πλευρὰν τόδε ἀρχαῖον
ἐπίγραμμα εὗρον.

ΘΕΟΙΣ
ΕΠΙ ΑΡΙΣΤΑΓΟΡΑ · ΑΡΧΟΝΤΟΣ
ΕΝ ΔΕΛΦΟΙΣ · ΠΥΛΑΙΑΣ · ΗΡΙ-
ΝΗΣ · ΙΕΡΟΜΝΗΜΟΝΟΥΝΤΩΝ
ΑΙΤΩΛΩΝ · ΠΟΛΕΜΑΡΧΟΥ
ΑΛΕΞΑΜΕΝΟΥ · ΔΑΜΩ-
ΝΟΣ.

10. f. 280 b (κθ : f. 8 b), X. ii. p. 339.

On Παλεῖς in Cephallenia : (C. I. G. 346).

περὶ δὲ τῆς παλέων πόλεως εἰς ἀθήνας τόδε ἐπίγραμμα εὗρον.

ΑΥΤΟΚΡΑΤΟΡΑ ΚΑΙΣΑΡΑ ΤΡΑΙΑ-
ΝΟΝ ΗΑΔΡΙΑΝΟΝ · ΣΕΒΑΣΤΟΝ ϙ
ΟΛΥΜΠΙΟΝ
ΠΟΛΙΣ ΠΑΛΕΩΝ ΤΗΣ ΚΕΦΑΛΛΑ-
ΝΙΑΣ · ΕΛΕΥΘΕΡΑ · ΚΑΙ · ΑΥΤΟΝΟ-
ΜΟΣ · ΔΙΑ ΕΠΙΜΕΛΗΤΟΥ · ΑΡΗΟΥ
ΦΙΛΟΥ · ΤΟΥ · ΑΓΑΘΟΚΛΕΟΣ · ΥΙΟΥ ·

Below this is a note in red :

ὅτι σάμον ὁ ποιητὴς καὶ τὴν σαμοθράκην λέγει.

Then in Cyriacus' hand :

Tℏ · Q · s · Q · N
s · Tℏ · F · ϙ

(i.e. Threiciamque Samum quae nunc Samothracia fertur. *Aen.* vii. 208).

ὡς λατίνων,
ποιητὴς φησὶ :

then in red :

Θρηΐκίαν τε σάμον ἡ νῦν
σαμοθράκια λέγεται.

There is a brief description of the MS. in Falconer's Oxford
Strabo (1807), I. pp. v, vi, and the text has been used throughout
that edition.

[C. M. A. 116.]

142. Bl. 4. 15.

XENOPHONTIS CYROPAEDEIA ET ANABASIS GRAECE.

Paper, 12 × 8, ff. 178, 29 lines to a page.   Cent. xiv. (?).   In a
fine hand.   Each book has a title ornamented in red.
Collation: $a^{10}-\iota^{10}$ ‖ $a^{10}-\zeta^{10}$ η^8 (8 blank).

Contents :

Xenophontis Cyropaedeia . . . . f.	1
στίχοι ιαμβικοί (xxx)	100 b
Xenophontis Anabasis	101

The iambic verses are mediaeval, and of a moral tendency :
they begin :

Inc.   οὐδέν τι τερπνὸν ὡς πάλαιός τις λόγος
          ἔχων τε λαμπρὰν τὴν ἀλήθειαν πᾶσαν.
Expl.   Ἔλθοις ἀνάσσων εὐτυχῶς αὐτοκράτωρ.

This MS. was used for the text of Hutchinson's edition of
the *Anabasis* in 1735, and is frequently quoted (from Hutchinson) e.g. by J. G. Schneider in his edition of the *Anabasis* (Oxford,
1821).   It was collated for Hutchinson by John Burton, Fellow
of Eton.
Doubtless given by Wotton.

[C. M. A. 126.]

143. Bl. 4. 16.

PHOTII LEXICON GRAECE.

Paper, 10⅝ × 8¾, ff. 166, written.   Cent. xviii.
Collation: A⁶ B⁸-T⁸ V⁸ X⁸, the rest blank.

This is a transcript from the Gale MS. now at Trinity College, Cambridge, together with an *Index auctorum* (ff. V 3 *b*-X 3 *a*).

There is a similar transcript among Richard Topham's books in this Library (marked Bf. 1. 1).

The present copy was given by Edw. Betham, Fellow, in 1773.

[C. M. A. *vac.*]

[For Bl. 5–12 see above under no. 49, p. 24.]

144. Bl. 5. 13.

S. ATHANASII SYNOPSIS, ETC., GRAECE.

Paper, 11¼ × 8½, ff. 256, varying numbers of lines to a page. Cent. xiv., xv. Bound in old patterned paper over paste-boards: two clasps. In quires of 8 leaves.

Contents:

1. Synopsis Sacrae Scripturae, attributed to S. Athanasius . . f. 1
   Σύνοψις ἐπίτομος τῆς θείας γραφῆς παλαιᾶς καὶ νέας διαθήκης...
   τοῦ ἁγίου καὶ μεγάλου Ἀθανασίου.

This tract was first printed at Heidelberg in 1600 among the works of Athanasius. Felckmann, the editor, says (Tom. ii. App. p. 84): Usae sunt operae textu huius Synopseos graece descripto ex vetusto et miris ductibus constante codice, quem ex bibliotheca viri clarissimi Petri Neveleti Doschii curavit vir ampliss. D. Bongarsius, etc.

Montfaucon, in his edition of Athanasius II. p. viii, says: Quorsum autem evaserit codex ille memoratus a Felkmanno, ignoratur. Codicem Synopseos aliquem nec vidi nec alicubi extare didici.

As the name F. N. Nevelet occurs on f. 1 of this MS. we may with great plausibility identify it with the copy used for the edition of 1600. It seems, therefore, to be the only known authority for the text of this interesting tract: on which see Zahn, *Gesch. d. NTlich Kanons*, II. 302 sqq. and Klostermann, *Analecta zur Septuaginta*. I hope soon to publish particulars of the text.

2. Dorothei Synopsis de Prophetis, de Apostolis, de lxxii Dis-
   cipulis 99
3. Σύνοψις χρονικὴ ἀπὸ Ἀδὰμ ἕως Ἀλεξίου τοῦ Κομνηνοῦ . . 129

It seems really to extend only as far as Cleopatra.

4. Synodicon 145

From the Apostolic Council to that of Nicaea.

5. Sophronii κατὰ πάσης αἱρέσεως liber 183
6. Anastasii περὶ πίστεως liber 219
7. Gelasii Cyziceni σύνταγμα τῶν ἐν Νικαίᾳ 241
8. Πρακτικὰ τῆς ἐν Ἐφέσῳ συνόδου 337
9. Nicephori Epistola ad Leonem 498

Ff. 1–120 are in one hand, with 35 lines to a page.
On f. 72 b (p. 144) is the note :

ἐγράφη γοῦν διὰ χειρὸς ἐμοῦ δουκᾶ νοταρίου,

and a similar note is on f. 73 a.

Ff. 121–168 are in another hand, in double columns of 29 lines each.

From f. 169 to the end we have Doukas's hand again, in double columns.

The colophon at the end of the volume is :

Τέλος σὺν θεῷ τῆς βίβλου ταύτης τῶν πρακτικῶν τῆς οἰκουμενικῆς τρίτης συνόδου.
Ἐτελειώθη γοῦν διὰ χειρὸς ἐμοῦ τοῦ ταπηνοῦ νοταρίου τῆς ἁγιωτάτης τοῦ θεοῦ μεγάλης ἐκκλησίας· διὰ συνδρομῆς καὶ ἐξόδου τοῦ ἁγιωτάτου καὶ καθολικοῦ τῆς συνόδου ἱερομονάχου φρᾶ. Ἰωάννου ἀπὸ τῆς ῥαγουζίας.

There was a John of Ragusa, who was Cardinal Abp of Argos, and died in 1418–19.

As to the owners of the MS. we have several indications. On f. 1, at the bottom, are these names :

(1) Ioannis......beneficio D. 1. 1550.
(2) F. N. Neueleti.
(3) Ex libris Danielis Mauclerc doct. iur. Victoriacensis (of Vitry-le-François) 1665 (? 1685).
(4) Ex libris Jac. Mauclerc, M.D., 1700.
(5) Ex libris Joh. Hen. Mauclerc, M.D., 1748.

The last-named has left several letters and notes about the contents of the book : he presented it to the Librarian of the College, the Rev. R. Huggett.

[C. M. A. vac.]

145. Bl. 5. 14.

S. AMBROSII QUAEDAM.

Vellum, $11\frac{1}{2} \times 7\frac{1}{2}$, ff. 89, 33 lines to a page. Cent. xii. Perhaps written in England: there are plain initials.

Collation: i^8–x^8 xi^8 (+ 1).

On f. 89 *b* is:

> sancti spiritus assit michi gratia amen.

Contents:

> S. Ambrosii liber de Isaac et anima.
> ,,   de fuga seculi.
> ,,   de Iacob et uita beata.
> ,,   de paradiso.
> Eiusdem apologia in regem Dauid.

The MS. belonged to Will. Horman.

[C. M. A. 9.]

146. Bl. 6. 1.

DIONYSII ORBIS PERIEGESIS CUM COMMENTARIO EUSTATHII GRAECE.

Paper, $8\frac{1}{4} \times 6$, ff. 232, 22 lines to a page. Cent. xv. In a clear hand.

Collation: a^8–δ^8 ‖ a^8–$\kappa\epsilon^8$.

Contents:

> Dionysii Periegesis   .   .   .   .   f. 1

It ends on f. 28.

> Eustathii commentarius   33

The leaves between the text and comment are blank. At the end is a monogram which I cannot decipher.

Doubtless given by Wotton.

[C. M. A. 51.]

147. Bl. 6. 2.

L. Apuleii Madaurensis Metamorphoseon Libri XI. et Florida.

Vellum, 8¾ × 6, ff. 123, 30 lines to a page: written in Italy. Cent. xv. (early).

Mended and rebound in 1894: it has suffered much both from damp and fire.

Collation: a¹⁰–d¹⁰ e⁸ f¹⁰–m¹⁰ n⁶ (wants 6).

On f. 122 *b* are the words:

> Codex Bernardi Bembi patricii Veneti,

and on f. 123 *a* are a few notes in the same hand. The MS. was no doubt given to the College by Sir Henry Wotton.

On f. 1 *a* is a very faint note, probably by Bembo, which seems to give the day of the month on which the book was bought. It reads:

> .... aged p... a .. pua. pro pal...
> modani · die · x. Julij · . v Ju.

Contents:

Metamorphoses s. Asinus Aureus . . . . f.   1
Florida 105

The interest of this book consists in a number of pen and ink drawings by an Italian artist, illustrative of the text, which occur, mostly on the bottom of the page, irregularly throughout the book. These drawings are of very high artistic value. They may be usefully compared with the drawings in a MS. in the Ambrosian Library at Milan, which has been reproduced in facsimile by Ceriani at the expense of Mr J. Gibson Craig, under the title of *Canonical Histories and Apocryphal Legends*. I append a description.

1. f. 1 *a*. Full-page drawing of a donkey, its head to *R*.: in black.

2. f. 1 *b*. Full-page drawing of Apuleius, seated, full-face: he is bearded, a fillet is round his head: he wears a cloak with embroidered border and morse, an under garment with a square patch of embroidery on the breast, and a band of embroidery running vertically down from the centre of it. In his lap is a book kept open by his *L*. hand: in his raised *R*. hand is a pen. He sits on a square seat without back or arms, raised on a step. A fine drawing.

3. f. 2 *b*. Two men in cloaks, with hoods and capes, ride side by side towards *L*. The nearer one turns and waves his *L*. hand to a horse (saddled) which follows from *R*. There are traces of a man in front of it.

Metam. I. 2. The narrator Lucius tending his horse : his two companions talking.

4. f. 3 *a*. On *L*. a horse standing saddled, head to *R*. : a man (the nearer of the two riders in no. 3) stands before it with hands joined, looking at a large bearded man seated on *R*., with hands joined on his stomach.

I. 6. Ecce Socratem contubernalem meum aspicio.

5. f. 3 *b*. (*a*) A house-wall. A woman, seen in profile, looks out of the door : Socrates (the bearded man of no. 4) stands in front. I. 7.

(*b*) The narrator (who appeared in no. 4) shakes hands with Socrates, who raises a garment before his face. I. 8.

6. f. 4 *a*. (*a*) On *L*. the narrator and Socrates sit facing one another on couches : a table and candlestick between them. I. 7.

(*b*) An old woman, in hood and long cloak, faces *R*., with hands raised : a crescent moon in the sky, between two stars : on the ground a large-mouthed pitcher : on *R*. a coiled serpent. I. 9.

7. f. 4 *b*. A room with two beds, foot to foot : between them a pitcher-like lamp hangs by three cords from the ceiling. The narrator is in the bed on *L*., leaning his head on his hands, with bent elbow. Socrates in bed on *R*., sleeping : neither is clothed. I. 11.

8. f. 5 *a*. (*a*) Socrates in bed, head to *L*. : two old women on the further side, at his head. They catch the blood from a wound in his throat in a basin. A turret is seen on the roof on *L*. : a niche with a jug in it, at the foot of the bed. I. 13.

(*b*) In front of an empty bed the narrator prostrate : the two old women maltreat him : an overturned stool on *R*. I. 13.

9. f. 5 *b*. Socrates in bed on *L*. On *R*. the narrator, with stick and bundle, walking, a porter in bed on the floor sits up and scolds, with raised hand : he has a night-cap : keys on a hook over his head. I. 14, 15.

10. f. 6 *a*. (*a*) The room : Socrates in bed : the narrator has fallen on him, with a broken rope round his neck. The end of the rope hangs from a pulley in the ceiling. I. 16, 17.

(*b*) The narrator faces *R*., with stick and bundle, says good bye to the porter : Socrates, behind him, leans on a stick : the outside of the door is seen : it is arched, and has a lock. I. 17 *sub fin*.

11. f. 6 *b*. (*a*) Narrator with stick and bundle : Socrates with stick, walking. I. 18.

(*b*) They sit, facing, on the ground : a tree between them, with a wallet hung on it : Socrates has a stick in his hand. Both eat. I. 19, *init*.

12. f. 7 *a*. (*a*) The narrator (beardless) faces *L*., and holds Socrates by the *L*. leg. Socrates is prostrate, with his face in a stream. I. 19 (§ 63).

(*b*) The narrator (face *R*.) digs with his stick in the ground. Socrates lies on his back behind him. I. 19.

13. f. 7 *b*. (*a*) Beardless man on horse faces *L*. : in front of a door, a woman with distaff meets him. I. 21.

(*b*) The same man on horse faces *R*., and talks to a man (it should be a maid) leaning out of window. Tower on roof. I. 22 (§ 68).

14. f. 8 *a*. On *L*. Lucius dismounted, in front of his horse, before a door, hands in a letter. Inside, a man and woman sit opposite to each other at table with bottle, tumbler and dish on it. She eats, he turns round and takes the letter. A maid (Fotis) stands with folded arms on *R*. I. 22 (§§ 69, 70).

15. f. 8 *b*. (*a*) Lucius, uncloaked, shakes hands with bearded man, who has long curling (Phrygian) cap; facing R., he points back with short staff. He is Pytheas. I. 24 (§§ 74, 75).

(*b*) Slave, with shaven head and short tunic, spills basket of fish on the ground : he stands in front of a table, on which are fish, square weights and scales. Behind it sits a man in round cap, with raised hands. I. 25 (§ 79).

16. f. 9 *a*. (*a*) Fotis, with long hair, faces *R*., and talks to Lucius, who is surprised : both his hands raised. I. 26 (§ 79).

(*b*) Lucius in bed, feet to *R*. Fotis enters from *R*., and puts on or pulls off the coverlet. I. 26 (§ 81).

17. f. 9 *b*. (*a*) Group of four : Lucius kneels on *R*., facing *R*., and is kissed by a stooping lady : two maids behind her converse. II. 2 (§§ 85 sqq.). The lady is Byrrhaena.

(*b*) Group of three : the first from *L*. is a man with beard and broad hat looking *L*. : his hand rests on the shoulder of (2), a man in curled cap, who looks *R*. at (3), a beardless youth in hat, facing *L*., his hand raised. II. 2 (§ 85).

18. f. 10 *a*. (*a*) Two maids walking.

(*b*) Lady leading Lucius.

(*c*) Man (no. 1 of 17 (*b*)) conducts them up steps : arched porch at top. Tower behind. II. 3, 4 (§§ 90, 91).

19. f. 10 *b*. (*a*) Lady (Byrrhaena) and Lucius sit on bench and talk.

(*b*) Outside, a man with hat and beard talks to a man with curled cap and man in high cap on *R*. : two maids, facing *L*., touch the latter. II. 5 (§§ 95, 96).

20. f. 11 *a*. Fotis stirs a pot on the fire, and beckons to Lucius, who enters on *R*. with one hand to mouth, and the other stretched out. II. 7 (§ 102).

21. f. 11 *b*. A room : on *L*. a man with beard and cap talks to his wife : a maid stands on *R*., face *L*. : a youth (Lucius) sits back to them on a stool by the fire (?), his head and hands raised. Outside, two curved objects on the wall (snakes or lizards) slightly converge towards the top. II. 11. (*Lacertam* was read for *lucernam* ?)

22. f. 12 *a*. (*a*) Lucius and Fotis stand and kiss each other.

(*b*) Lucius, facing *R*., greets a slave (?) with stick, who points with his thumb over his shoulder at a man behind holding out three cocks.

23. f. 12 *b*. A man and wife sit talking on a bench : a maid stands behind them, facing *R*. : a square niche in the wall with a vessel in it : a dog looks *R*. at Lucius and a bearded man in cap, sitting and talking on an angle-bench. II. 11, 12.

24. f. 13 *a*. Lucius looks up to *R*., and addresses a bearded man with turban, open book in his *R*. hand, his *L*. hand pointing up : he sits on a high seat with a step in front : on *R*. a small square pedestal, on which a bearded man places money : on *R*. of it a crowd looking on and talking. II. 13 (§ 110) Milo's story of Diophanes, the weather-prophet, being cheated of his money.

25. f. 13 *b*. (*a*) Lucius in bed : at foot, on *R*., stands Fotis, wreathed with roses, and scattering roses on the coverlet from her lap.

(*b*) Lucius and Fotis in bed, feet to *R*. : in front, jug, bottle and tub. II. 16 (§ 127).

26. f. 14 *a*. Lucius (a youth) on *L*., faces *R*., and talks to a man with long robe, beard, and hat in hand, who approaches with bent knee, and takes his hand. Behind them a man with long curling cap, and hand raised, girt with a scymitar.

(*b*) Youth, with sword held point upward, faces *R*. Opposite to him a man stands talking. (§ 134.)

27. f. 14 b. A banquet scene. On L., a table with bottle, and jugs, and goblets : a large pitcher on the floor in front. Behind it, a man pours from a round-bellied bottle into a goblet. On R., an attendant in tight clothes, with hand raised, and jug in L. hand. In centre, the banquet table, with dishes, knives, etc. Three people : (1) the host, bearded, (2) Lucius, (3) the wife, sit full-face : 1 and 2 talk : 2 has knife and bread, 3 talks to the bearded attendant of 26 (a), who wears a high cap. II. 20 (§ 135 sqq.).

28. f. 15 a. A man, with long beard and robe, sits, face R.: a man stands talking to him, holding a knotted stick, and points to his breast : he wears a short tunic.

(b) Under a thatched booth, a woman sits full-face : by her are three plaited baskets containing crockery. A man on R. takes a jug and puts money into her hand : another, with basket on head, stands by.

(c) A man, facing R., sits under a shelter. Before him is a table, with a round object and money on it : a man with a cap, peaked in front, talks to him, and points to two dogs behind.

29. f. 15 b. (a) A woman with her hair down sits on the ground and rends her clothes. There enter from R. two men, (1) bearded, in long robe, (2) with short dress and staff.

(b) A woman stands at the foot of a bed, facing R. In the bed is a corpse, nude, with arms crossed on the coverlet, head to right. The woman is agitated. Behind the bed stands the man with staff, talking. At the head of the bed are the bearded man and a crowd of six people behind him. II. 23.

ff. 16–23 have no pictures.

30. f. 24 a. (a) Donkey, with human head, bearded, standing on its hind-quarters. Fotis, face R., holds his front legs.

(b) Donkey faces L., kicking out his hind legs : behind him Fotis weeps and rends her clothes. III. 24.

31. f. 24 b. (a) A horse feeds out of a manger, facing R. Opposite to it, two donkeys : one haltered feeds, the other (Lucius) comes up prancing. III. 26.

(b) Man with short clothes and stick beats Lucius, who, on his hind legs, tries to eat a wreath of roses at the top of a pillar. III. 27.

32. f. 25 a. (a) An armed man has cut a hole in the lid of a chest with an adze, or mattock, and takes out a bag. The chest is under a canopy ; a turret above.

(b) Six armed men, with swords and shields and pointed helmets, march off with plunder. III. 28.

33. f. 25 b. The same armed men drive in front of them two donkeys and a horse, or mule, with packs across their backs. III. 28.

ff. 26–31 have no pictures.

34. f. 32 a. A maiden, full-faced, in the midst of an armed band of eight men, who seize her. Her hair is long, her head inclined to R. An old woman sits on a bank under a tree, facing L. IV. 23.

35. f. 36 b. Unfinished : a figure sits facing R., with hand raised as if talking. IV. 27 (?).

ff. 37–51 a have no pictures.

36. f. 51 b. (a) Donkey tethered, braying, throws up his heels.

(b) Maiden in front, mounted on donkey. VI. 27.

37. f. 52 a. Maiden on donkey : wooded slope in front, with a deer looking out from among trees. Four roads meet in the centre.

38. f. 53 *b*. The old woman sits under rock, facing *R*. Band of robbers, a youth among them, sit facing *R*. A countryman in cloak, and hat with peak on front, stands opposite talking.

39. f. 54 *a*. Donkey couching, tethered to a manger, looks up : head to *L*.

40. f. 54 *b*. Old woman hanging from tree. Robber, facing *L*., with mace, leads maiden on donkey : the band follow. VI. 30.

41. f. 59 *b*. Catchword of quire : a fish done in red, with four back fins, swallowing a smaller fish.

42. f. 69 *b*. A flagon, in red, with a chalice at its lip.

43. f. 79 *b*. Dog with collar : badly copied on the opposite page.

44. f. 89 *b*. Ostrich, in black and red : a horse-shoe in its beak.

45. f. 106 *b*. An eagle, in black : a crown on its head, something in its beak. *Florida*, I. 2.

46. f. 107 *a*. Half-length, a bearded man, full-face, helmeted, blowing two long trumpets. (Hyagnis, father of Marsyas.) I. 3.

47. f. 107 *b*. Marsyas lies on his back, bearded, staff or pipe in his *R*. hand. Four Muses—represented as hooded women—stand at his head : one holds his *L*. wrist and flays the arm with a knife. Five Muses at his feet : one flays his *R*. leg with a knife. I. 3.

48. f. 108 *b*. A king, bearded, on canopied throne, faces *R*. Five men are before him : three are bearded : one with long beard and robe talks to him. I. 7. Alexander, Polycletus, Apelles, Pyrgoteles, Apuleius (?), Clemens (?).

49. f. 109 *b*. Elephant, with trunk curling outwards : hairs on his body marked in red.

Colophon : f. 119 *b* :

Finito libro sit laus et gloria Christo.

On f. 122 *b* are Bembo's name, and the Greek alphabet and *Gloria patri* in Greek transliterated.

[C. M. A. 12.]

148. Bl. 6. 3.

GEORGII ETHRIGII CONIURATIO WIATI SUB MARIA REGINA.

Paper, 5⅝ × 4, ff. 35 + 4 blank, 7 lines to a page. Cent. xvi.

It is a poem in Greek hexameters, dedicated to Queen Mary, by the author, at Oxford, IV. Non. Apr.

There is a Latin preface : the poem consists of about 370 lines.

[C. M. A. *vac.*]

149. Bl. 6. 4.

M. T. Ciceronis de Officiis Libri iii.

Vellum, 6 × 4, ff. 127, 25 lines to a page. Cent xv. (1497). Written at Rome ; in a beautiful hand.

Collation : A^{10}–M^{10} N^8 (7 cancelled, 8 blank).

Colophon : in capitals, red, blue and gold :

M. T. Ciceronis officiorum lib. finit.   Romae die Martis xiv Februari MCCCCLXXXXVII. B. S.

F. 1 *a* is a beautiful piece of work. The text is written in alternate lines of blue and gold. The border is classical, with columns, on the bases of which are blank shields. At the bottom is a painting of four sages, seated, disputing. The initial has a picture of Cicero, bearded, seated, and talking to his son.

Doubtless given by Wotton. It much resembles a MS. of Horace, which also belonged to Wotton, and is now in the Library of King's College (no. 34).

[C. M. A. 119.]

150. Bl. 6. 5.

Theodulus, Maximianus, etc.

Vellum, 9 × 6½, ff. 81, 29 lines to a page. Cent. x., xi. In Lombardic minuscules.

Collation : a^8 (wants 1–7) b^8–l^8.

1. Theoduli Ecloga . . . . f. 1

It is a dialogue in hexameters between Pseustis and Alethia, with Fronesis for umpire. The author lived in the xth century (at Athens), and his poem has been often printed, e.g. by J. Schwabe, Altenberg, 1773.

This copy is imperfect : it begins

> Si uictus fueris non me uicisse fateris
> Sed quia mutari nescit sentencia cepti
> En adaquare greges simul et releuare calorem
> Nostra uenit fronesis · sedeat pro iudice nobis.

2. Maximiani Elegiae vi. . . . . 6 *b*

These are the Elegies formerly attributed to Cornelius Gallus.

See two papers by Professor Robinson Ellis: *On the Elegies of Maximianus* in the *American Journal of Philology*, 1884, pp. 1–15 and 145–163. Bährens has used the MS. for his text of Maximianus in the *Poetae Latini Minores*: it is apparently the earliest and best MS. extant.

There is a peculiar feature about this copy. F. 6 *b* opens with the end of Theodulus' Eclogue, thus:

> [320]   Sol petit oceanum, frigus succedit opacum
> Desine quod restat ne desperacio ledat
>
>   E
> BAXLE .·, DAMA .·, IACN · USNANSA
>
> Emula quid cessas finem properare senectus
> Cur et in hoc fesso corpore tarda uenis.

The capital E belongs probably to the Eclogue; it may be a mistake for an F, the initial of Fronesis, for the initials of the interlocutors are placed at the end of the lines throughout the poem. The enigmatical line that follows, might, I have thought, be a corrupt form of the title of the Elegies that follow: and the name Maximianus may be concealed therein.

> 3. P. P. Statii Achilleis   29

Readings from this MS. are given by Dr Karl Schenkl.

> 4. P. Ouidii Nasonis liber de remedio amoris   38
> 5.   ,,   Epistolae (Heroides i. 7–vii. 159)   .   .   52

Used by Mr E. S. Shuckburgh in his edition of the *Heroides*.

> 6. Aratoris subdiaconi Historia Apostolica   71

Ends with i. 521:

> Erumpensque dies alieno tempore sanctos.

Most probably given by Wotton.

                                        [C. M. A. 101.]

151.   Bl. 6. 6.

Io. Baptistae Mantuani Secunda Parthenice.

Vellum, 8⅜ × 5½, ff. 48, 27 lines to a page. Cent. xv. Written in Italy: a beautiful MS.

Collation: a¹⁰ b⁸–e⁸ f⁶ (4–6 blank).

Contents :

1. Some verses and an extract from S. Hieronymus ad Deme-
triadem : in Bern. Bembo's hand (?) . . . . . f. 1
2. De fratre Baptista Mantuano carmen Petri Bembi Bernardi filii 2 b

Ten lines in purple ink : two corrections seem to be in Bernardo Bembo's hand.

3. Letter from Jo. Bapt. Mantuanus to B. Bern. Bembus patricius
Venetus Iurisconsultus . . . . 3 a

The initial has in it the words IN DEO SALUTARI MEO, and branches of bay and palm. In the lower margin are Bembo's arms, with similar branches, and a motto, VIRTVS ET HONOR.

4. Argument of the Poem . . . . 4 a
5. The Poem Secunda Parthenice, on S. Katherine.

It is followed by a copy of Elegiacs by Franc. Caeretus of Parma, Juris Pontificii scholaris, addressed *in Inuidum Lectorem.*

Colophon :

Secundae Parthenices opus diuinum Bononie impressum solerti animaduersione Franc. Cereti permensis communibus impensis Benedicti Hectoris Bibliopolae Platonisque eiusdem impressoris accuratissimi ciuium bononiensium anno natiuitatis dominicae M · CCCC · LXXIX · Quinto die Februarii.

Doubtless given by Wotton.

[C. M. A. 94.]

152. Bl. 6. 7.

IUVENALIS SATIRAE.

Vellum, $8\frac{1}{8} \times 5\frac{1}{4}$, ff. 66, 30 lines to a page. Cent. xv. Written in Italy.

Collation : i^{10}–v^{10} vi^6. Text ends on 64 a.

There are notes at the end in Bern. Bembo's writing, giving the subjects of the Satires, etc. Sat. i. has a very good initial.

The margins are cut. A running title extends as far as Sat. ix. After the text is YHS MARIA, and three blank pages.

Doubtless from Wotton.

[C. M. A. 85.]

153. Bl. 6. 8.

IUVENALIS ET PERSII SATIRAE.

Vellum, 6¾ × 4, ff. 92 + 4, 25 lines to a page. Cent. xv.
Written in Italy, in a beautiful hand, resembling that of B. Bembo.
Collation: i¹⁰–ix¹⁰ x²; 4 fly-leaves.
The Satires of Persius begin on f. 79.
At the bottom of f. 1, an angel holding the shield of Bembo.
There are notes in B. Bembo's writing at the end.
The Satires of Juvenal are divided into five books, with argu-
ments in hexameters, and titles in red.
No doubt given by Wotton.

[C. M. A. 86.]

154. Bl. 6. 9.

COMMENTARIUS IN PERSII SATIRAS.

Paper, 8¼ × 5⅝, ff. 62, 24 lines to a page. Cent. xvi. Written
in Italy: quite a plain MS.
Collation: A⁸–G⁸ H⁶.

Inc. Aulus Persius Flaccus natus est pridie non. dec.
Expl. Ut qui auaritie eius finem uoluerit imponere facile uideatur et syllogismum
Chrysippi deffinire.

No doubt from Wotton.

[C. M. A. 105.]

155. Bl. 6. 10.

EUTROPII HISTORIA CUM CONTINUATIONE PAULI DIACONI.

Paper, 7⅞ × 5½, ff. 80, 35 lines to a page. Cent. xv., xvi. In
an upright Italian hand, with initials in pen and ink.
Collation: i¹²–vi¹² vii⁸.
No doubt from Wotton.

[C. M. A. 52, 103.]

156. Bl. 6. 11.

PAULI MARSI PIERII PISCINATIS BEMBICE PEREGRINE.

Vellum, $8\frac{3}{4} \times 4\frac{3}{4}$, ff. 40 + 2, 18 lines to a page. Cent. xv. In an Italian hand.

Collation: a² i¹⁰–iv¹⁰ : text ends on f. 35 *a*.

On f. 1 *b* is Bembo's motto, VIRTUS ET HONOR, surrounded by bay and palm.

On f. 2 *a* are Bembo's arms in a red ribbon, and the title of the poem, and an address of the author to his book.

The contents are poems by " Paulus Marsius, ex Argolica Profectione (here is inserted in green, by Bembo, *uocatus ac demum*) inuitatus ad Hispalicam " (added, *ad B. Bembum in hispania legatum*).

There are also Poems addressed to the Virgin—to the Senate and people of Syracuse, who feared the plague, and would not let the author land—to Cronicus ; and verses written at Malta, on the sight of Carthage, at Hippo (dated 28 Aug. 1477).

At the end are five blank leaves : on the last is this note (of an election at Venice) :

pro censor.	Cos.	et	Triumuiratu	
Bembus	82..	417		
Jo. Maurotus	798	444		
Donatus	606	644		13 Julii 1494.
Lauredanus	309	936		
Sanutus	650	593		
Grimaldus	634	646		

No doubt from Wotton.

[C. M. A. 95.]

157. Bl. 6. 12.

NALDI DE NALDIS BUCOLICA.

Vellum, $8\frac{1}{4} \times 5$, ff. 32, 20 lines to a page. Cent. xv. In an Italian hand.

Collation: a⁴ b¹⁰ c¹⁰ d⁸.

Contents:

1. Naldi Naldii Florentini epigramma ad clarissimum Virum
    Bernardum Bembum legatum Venetum .   .   .   .   f. 3 *b*
2. Naldi de Naldis Bucolica in Laurentium Mediceum Iuuenem
    clarissimum. Daphnis. Aegloga in Laurentium eundem
    (in gold capitals)   4

This page is finely bordered : in the initial is Daphnis chasing
a nymph. In the lower margin are the Medici arms, with the
lilies in the centre.

There are xi. Eclogues.

Given doubtless by Wotton.

[C. M. A. 99.]

158.   Bl. 6. 13.

Io. Boccacius de Mulieribus claris.

Paper, $8\frac{3}{8} \times 5\frac{1}{2}$, ff. 96, 31 lines to a page. Cent. xv. In an
Italian hand, well-written, and quite plain. There are some
scribbles in Greek on the last page.

Collation: $i^{10}-ix^{10}$ x^6.

No doubt from Wotton.

[C. M. A. 33.]

159.   Bl. 6. 14.

A Poem in Italian, without title.

Paper, $8\frac{1}{2} \times 5\frac{3}{4}$, ff. 70 + 1 blank, 14 lines to a page. Cent. xvi.,
xvii.

Inc.   Vanne libello mio uanne filui
        Chio scio che anderai in assai gente
        Ma se alcun mai Ti mordera con dente
        Sapia che udio sol errar non lui.

The hand resembles that of the *Musae admirantes* (see no. 174).
From Wotton.

[C. M. A. *vac.*]

160. Bl. 6. 15.

TRACTATUS DE PHYSICIS, ETC.

Vellum, 6¾ × 4⅜, ff. 26 + 2, 29 lines to a page. Cent. xiv. (It is said to bear the date 1497, but I was unable to find this.)

It is a fragment, consisting of 2 quires of 10 leaves, numbered xxii and xxiii, and 1 of 6 leaves, numbered xxiiii: the leaves are numbered 204–227.

Contents:

1. *Inc.* modo siccum ex uicinitate estatis modo eadem ratione
   calidum modo frigidum . . . . f. 1

With diagrams of the changes of the Moon, and of eclipses.

2. De eis que agit relatus a firmamento . . . . . . 2 *b*
3. De eclipsi solis . . . . 3 *b*
4. Capitula tercie particule . . . . 5 *b*
   1. De aere.
      Quae v^que zone sunt in aere non in ethere.

There are 26 chapters: the last is:

   Unde sit quod in lunacione modo crescunt humores, modo
   decrescunt.
5. Capitula quarte particule (38 in number) . . . . . 12 *b*
   1. De diversis qualitatibus terre.
   38. De iuuentute et senectute et senio.

The end is complete:

   ...non enim extincto naturali calore diu potest homo uiuere.

At the end are two supplementary leaves, in paler ink, containing:

(*a*) Twenty-two hexameter verses on the names of Christ . f. 1
   Inc. Omnipotens dominus ih̄c xp̄c deus altus.
(*b*) The beginnings of the four Gospels 2
(*c*) A rhyming hymn 3

   deus magnus et immensus
   et quem nullus capit sensus
   deus iudex equitatis.

(*d*) An adjuration, partly erased, against all dangers . . 3 *b*
   A prayer against evil spirits.
(*e*) Ps. cvii. (cviii.) 4

[C. M. A. *vac.*]

161.   Bl. 6. 16.

ADELARDUS BATONIENSIS DE SOLUTIONE QUAESTIONUM NATURALIUM.

Vellum, 6⅝ × 4⅜, ff. 37, 30 lines to a page.   Cent. xii.
Collation : a⁸–d⁸ e⁷⁸ (wants 6–8).
The last two leaves have suffered much from damp, before they were in their present binding (of cent. xviii.).

Contents :

Incipit liber Adelardi Batoniensis ad nepotem suum de solucione
questionum naturalium   .   .   .   .   f. 1

The title is not in the original hand.   The tract is imperfect, ending :

... Quidam autem altius uel intelligentes uel furentes ...

There are tags on the margins of the leaves, written by the original scribe.   In the opinion of Mr Holmes, the Queen's Librarian, this is very probably Adelard's autograph MS.   (Rev. H. St J. Thackeray, *Eton College Library*, p. 14.)   Tanner in the *Bibliotheca Britannica*, s. v. Athelardus mentions this MS.

Adelard's date was 1130 (Bale, i. p. 183).

[C. M. A. 1.]

162.   Bl. 6. 17.

TRADITIONS ILLUSTRATIVE OF PASSAGES IN THE KORAN: IN ARABIC.

Paper, 8 × 5¾, ff. 29, 15 lines to a page.   Cent. xvii. (?).   Mutilated at both ends.
Collation : a¹⁰ b¹⁰ c⁸ (+ 1).
Written in the Maghrik character.

[C. M. A. *vac.*]

163. Bl. 6. 18.

VITA ALEXANDRI MAGNI GRAECOBARBARA.

Paper, $8\frac{1}{4} \times 5\frac{1}{2}$, ff. 209, 20 lines to a page. Cent. xvi. Bound in green velvet.

Collation: a^8–κ^8 $\kappa a^{(12+1)}$ $\kappa\beta^8$–$\kappa\delta^8$ $\kappa\epsilon^{12}$.

Title: Ἡ γέννησις καὶ διήγησις τοῦ ἀλλεξάνδρου μακεδώνων τὸ πῶς ἐγεννήθη· καὶ ἀνεθράφη καὶ τὸ πῶς εἶχεν τὴν ἀνδρίαν καὶ τὴν μάθησιν καὶ τὴν χάριταν ἀπὸ τὴν ἀρχήν.

Inc. Ἦτον ἀπὸ θεοῦ ὁρισμὸς καὶ ἦτον φρόνιμος καὶ εὔμορφος καὶ εἰς τοὺς αὐθέντας καὶ εἰς τὴν στρατίαν.

Colophon: Τῷ μεγαλειοτάτῳ καὶ πανεντιμοτάτῳ αὐθέντι καὶ ἀνδρικοτάτῳ καὶ αἰδεσιμοτάτῳ δεσπότῃ (⟩⟨ .)

Very likely from Wotton.

[C. M. A. 123.]

164. Bl. 6. 19.

THE ANATOMIE OF SPAYNE BY HARYE BEDWOD, GENT., 1599.

Paper, $9\frac{1}{4} \times 6\frac{3}{4}$, pp. 348, 22 lines to a page. 1599.

The title-page has an ornamented border, with coats of arms, all very neatly blazoned. At the top are the arms of Spain, and at the sides, those of the six provinces: under them is written :

FEARE SVSPICION | BASTARDIE | MVRTHER | TIRANIE | VSVRPACION | HIPOCHRESIE | PERIVRIE.

The book contains folding tables of pedigrees. The last page has a good coloured drawing of a peacock standing on a pomegranate : the eyes in its tail are coats of arms, and a scroll in Spanish is in its mouth.

[C. M. A. *vac.*]

165. Bl. 6. 20.

MAPHEI VEGII QUAEDAM.

Paper, $8\frac{5}{8} \times 5\frac{3}{4}$, ff. 119, 25 lines to a page ; in a running Italian hand. Cent. xv. (1444).

Collation: a^{12}–g^{12} ‖ h^{12} i^{12} k^{12} (12 cancelled).

Contents :

1. Mapheus Vegius de liberis educandis . . . . . . f. 1
    Inc. Si tantum nobis ingenii esset....

Colophon : f. 84 *b*

Ex libris clarissimi viri Vehii laudensis de liberorum educatione Epithoma feliciter finis adest.

Rome apud Sanctum petrum nono Kal. Januarij MCCCCXLIIII. tempus quo Mafeus librum feliciter edidit.

2. Contentio inter terram, aurum et solem de prestantia coram
    Joue per Mafeum 85
    Inc. Cum decertarent inter se aliquando.

Ends on 119 *a*.
Doubtless from Wotton.

[C. M. A. 96.]

166. Bl. 6. 21.

DEMONSTRATIO FRANCISCI FRATRIS ORD. MIN. CYPRII DE PURGATORIO GRAECE.

Paper, $8\frac{7}{8} \times 6\frac{1}{2}$, ff. 22, 19 lines to a page. Cent. xv., xvi.
Collation : a¹² b¹⁰.

Demonstratio Purgatorii e Scriptis Doctorum Ecclesiae.

Ἀναγνώστῃ τῷ ἐν χ͞ω ἀγαπητῷ.

Ἐπειδήπερ πολλοὶ ἐν τῇ πόλει ἀλλὰ καὶ ἐν τῇ νήσῳ (i.e. Cyprus) ταύτῃ εἰσὶν οἱ ἀντι-λέγονται πῦρ καθαρτήριον μετὰ τόνδε τὸν βίον μὴ εἶναι.

Colophon (in red):

Μνήσθητί μου τοῦ συλλέξαντος ταῦτα τὰ ἄνω ἅπαντα Φρανκίσκου τοῦ ἁμαρτωλοῦ τῆς τῶν μικροτέρων τάξεως ἱερομοναχοῦ ταπεινοῦ τοῦ κυπρίου.

The principal author quoted is Chrysostom. Also Athanasius, Epiphanius, Basil, Dionysius Areop., Cyril, Gregory Naz., Gregory Nyss., Theodoricus (*sic*) Κυρηναῖος.
Doubtless from Wotton.

[C. M. A. 53.]

167. Bl. 6. 22.

LIFE OF SIR THOMAS MORE.

Paper, $7\frac{3}{4} \times 6$, ff. 74, 22 lines to a page. Cent. xvi. Given by Franc. Goode, A.M. 1731.

The life, araignment, and death, of the famous learned Sir Thomas More, Knight, sometimes Lord Chancellor of England.

On the fly-leaf is:

hunc librum perlegi Ottuell Meuerell.

This title is in a border of natural flowers, without background. An engraved portrait (half-length) three-quarters full, turned to *L*.: holding a roll, ded. to Gosuin Batson of Brabant, is stuck on the verso.

f. 2. Dedication by William Hill to Simon Gearing.

[C. M. A. vac.]

168. Bl. 6. 23.

Paper, $6\frac{1}{4} \times 3\frac{7}{8}$, ff. circa 50 written, many blank. Cent. xviii.

Binding, red leather with gold tooling, and the Royal arms in gold. Given by Edw. Bp of Chichester (Waddington).

"Remembrances for order and Decency to be kept in the upper House of Parliament by the Lords when his Majesty is not there."

They are all dated, and range from about 1610 to 4 Mar. 1727.

[C. M. A. vac.]

169. Bl. 6. 24.

PETRI DE RIGA AURORA.

Vellum, $9 \times 5\frac{3}{8}$, ff. 179, 45 lines to a page. Cent. xii. or xiii. (early). In a good hand, probably English. Red and blue initials: one narrow column of text.

Collation: 1^8–22^8 23^4 (4 cancelled). Text ends on f. 177.

The *Aurora* is a paraphrase of the several books of the Bible in Latin verse.

Job follows Acts, and precedes Canticles.

Among other scribbles on the fly-leaf is :

"Eleyson Willelmus permissione diuina Caninarum Episcopus Aug.... apostolice sedis legatus Walterus."

[C. M. A. 32.]

170.   Bl. 6. 25.

Pharetra Sacramenti, contra Lollardos.

Vellum, $7\frac{1}{4}$ × 5, ff. 128, 24 lines to a page.   Cent. xv.   Written in England.   In quires of 16 leaves.

Fly-leaves :

1.   On Optics, with scribbled notes.
2.   Part of a Letter of Fraternity of Friars Minors dated circa festum Nativitatis B. V. M. at S. Bot(ulf), 1372.
Another on the same parchment, Dat. apud Leek in festo S. Michaelis.

The outside of the sheet is covered with writing in English.

Contents :

Incipit prologus in libellum editum contra lollardos qui dicitur Pharetra Sacramenti. Quis dabit capiti meo aquam.

It contains narratives of miracles of the Sacrament : one is dated 1424.

[C. M. A. 92.]

171.   Bl. 6. 26.

Nic. Gorrami Themata.

Vellum, $5\frac{3}{4}$ × $4\frac{5}{8}$, ff. 268, in double columns of 36 lines each. Cent. xiv., xv.
Collation : 1^{12} (wants 3, 4)–10^{12} ‖ 11^{12}–14^{12} 15^{10} 16^{12}–22^{12} ‖ 23^{8}.

Contents :

Incipiunt themata de dominicis edita per fr. Nycholaum de Gorram
   ordinis fratrum predicatorum   .   .   .   . f.   1

Ff. 119 *b*, 120 are blank.

Themata de festis   121
Index (perhaps by Horman), in a hand that has numbered the
   leaves of the MS.   261

[C. M. A. 63.]

172.　Bl. a. 1 (Bo. 3. 20).

IOANNES DE DONDIS PHYSICUS PADUANUS DE CONFICIENDIS
HOROLOGIIS OMNIUM PLANETARUM.

Paper, 13½ × 9½, ff. 58 + 87, two volumes in one.　Cent. xv.

Copied from another MS. of the date 1397 (see f. 1 of the text): written in Italy.

Part I., ff. 58.　Containing drawings of the various parts of planetary clocks.　They are most carefully and well done.

In quires of 10 leaves, and 1 of 8.

Part II., ff. 87.　The text to the above drawings, entitled, " opus planetarii Joanis de Dondis fisici paduani ciuis ": with further drawings, some of which are unfinished.

In quires of 8 and 10 leaves.

Colophon :

> Finito libro frangamus ossa magistro
> Finito a di 12 aprilis hora 21 o meza.

In the Bodleian is a MS. of this work dated 1461 (Cod. Laud. Miscell. 620).　The author constructed a clock still existing in a tower at Padua.

Very probably from Wotton.

[C. M. A. 54.]

173.　Bl. a. 2 (Bo. 7. 2).

GESTA IUDICUM ISRAELITICORUM A GEORGIO CASO.

Paper, 6 × 4, ff. xv + 2 blank.　Cent. xvii.

It is a hexameter poem (the song of Deborah is in elegiacs) dedicated to Robert Devereux, Earl of Essex, by George Case, " verbi praeco et minister," at Boxley, in Kent.

No doubt from Wotton, who was a Kentish man.

[C. M. A. *vac.*]

174. Bl. a. 3 (Bo. 3. 14).

Musae Admirantes.

Paper, 12½ × 9, ff. xvii + 2 blank. Cent. xvii. (1619).
The full title is :

Musae Admirantes Suspicientesque Illustrissimum et Excellentissimum Virum
DN. DN. HENRICVM WOTTONVM Anglo-Cantianum Inuictissimi et maximi illius JACOBI
Magnae Britanniae, Scotiae, et Hyberniae, etc., Regis, secundo Apud Serenissimam
Venetorum Rempublicam Legatum et Oratorem Amplissimum, submissi obseruantis
officiosique animi contestandi igitur, in publicum proscenium uariis carminibus pro-
ductae, a J. Petro Lotichio Hanonico, Med. et C. P. Caesar. S.

They are nine poems addressed to Sir H. Wotton, when ambassador at Venice for the second time, with Preface and " celeusma."
Wotton no doubt gave them to the Library.

[C. M. A. *vac.*]

175. Bl. a. 4 (Bo. 7. 24).

List of the Gentry in the Counties of England and Wales.

Paper, 16 × 6¼, ff. 74, in vellum wrapper. Cent. xvii. (1611).

Inc. Bedford.
    Thomas dominus Ellesmere Cancellarius Anglie.

The date (1611) may be gathered from the fact that Richard
Canterbury (Abp Bancroft, 1604–1611) and George Canterbury
(Abp Abbott, 1611–1633) are both mentioned.

[C. M. A. *vac.*]

176. Bl. a. 5.

Henrici de Bracton Liber de legibus Angliae.

Vellum, 11 × 8, ff. 289 + 10 of index, in double columns of 48
lines each. Cent. xiii. Written in England: rubricated initials,
inserted slips.

Collation : a¹⁰ b¹², etc.: the last of two leaves.

[C. M. A. *vac.*]

177.

FIGURAE BIBLIORUM.
APOCALYPSIS CUM FIGURIS.

Vellum, $10\frac{7}{8} \times 7\frac{1}{2}$, ff. 58, two volumes in one. Cent. xiii. Written in English: binding of cent. xvii., rebacked (1894).

Given to the College by George Henry Pitt, Esq., May 28th, 1817. On f. 8 *b* is:

> The gift of Sr John Sherard of Lobthorp in Lincolnshire.
> Stuart Bickerstaffe 1690.

Collation: a² b⁶ ‖ c⁸–h⁸ i².

The first eight leaves contain a series of paintings arranged in medallions, five and two halves on each page, of Scripture subjects, principally types and antitypes. They recall very strongly the painted windows of the thirteenth century, and I am strongly inclined to believe that they were actual designs for stained glass windows. I append a full description:

I. f. 1 *a*. Blank.

f. 1 *b*. Ground of the page blue: of the medallions red. These two colours alternate in the succeeding pages.

1. *Centre.* Creation of the world: Christ in bluish-green robe over brown, blue-crossed nimbus, scales in *L.* hand, compasses in *R.*, traces a sphere in the air, with three bands on it, in one is a snake (or a river), in the second trees, in the third fish. At the top of the picture are two demi-angels.

2. Bottom *R.* Creation of Beasts: Christ: on *L.*, lions, horse, dogs (?): on *R.*, a goat eats a tree.

3. Top *R.* Creation of Birds.

4. Top *L.* Creation of Adam: a line joins Christ's hand to Adam's mouth: tree on *R.*

5. Bottom *L.* Creation of Eve: a tree behind.

6. Half-circle on *L.* Man (prophet) in green, seated, in hood: hand raised: the end of a scroll, or garment, depends over his other hand: red folds are under his feet.

7. Half-circle on *R.* Beardless (?) man in green and pink: much damaged. He is seated, facing *L.*: one hand over his head: a scroll (?) on his knee.

II. f. 2 *a*.

1. *Centre.* The Prohibition (?). Christ, cross-nimbed, between two trees: on *L.*, a man in red robe over green, bearded, seated, hand raised. Christ has both hands raised.

2. Top *L.* The Temptation. The Serpent has a human head. Eve holds two apples.

3. Top *R.* The Expulsion. The Angel has two wings only, and a flaming sword: Adam and Eve with fig-leaves.

4. Bottom *L*. Toil. Adam on *L*., in light-coloured robe, striped, digs: a goat eats the leaves of a tree in *centre*: two sheep feed on *L*. of it. On *R*., facing L., Eve seated, with distaff and spindle.

5. Bottom *R*. Death of Abel. Abel in brown, prostrate on green rock. Cain on *R*. in red, with black legs, strikes him on the head with a jaw-bone. Behind, in air, are two sheaves (?) (each has a band round it) flaming: that on *L*. flames upwards, that on *R*. downwards.

6, 7. *L*. and *R*. Two adoring angels, full-length.

f. 2 *b* is blank.

III.   f. 3 *a*.

Here begins the series of types and prophecies, surrounding an antitype in the central medallion: the two half-circles, and the lower medallion on *L*., contain prophets, of whom only those in the whole medallion bear inscribed scrolls. The central medallion is supported by an atlas-figure, seated, of a Virtue, sometimes with name attached. On the lower margin is written one of the commandments. In some cases a green leaf-ornament connects the upper medallions with the central one.

Virtue, throned, in white and green, holds a white branch. *Caritas*.

Commandment. Non facies tibi sculptile neque adorabis deos alienos.

1. *Centre*. The Nativity. The Virgin in bed in front, her head to *L*., points with *L*. hand, and leans her head on her *R*. hand. Above her are turrets. In the centre, Christ swaddled lies in the manger, cross-nimbed: behind are the ox and ass. On *R*. Joseph seated, head on *R*. hand, stick in *L*. hand, not nimbed. Above, the star: at top, two demi-angels, probably holding the star.

Inscription (on the circular frame):

Nascitur eternus, virgo parit, ordo supernus
? n
Pangit, arabsque uehit: nuncia stella preit.

2, 3. Half-circles: two kneeling men with hands joined.

4. Top *L*. "Daniel's" vision of the stone cut without hands. Daniel asleep in a green bed, his head under a crocketed niche with a finial: head on hand, to *L*. In the centre, in air, a square block inscribed *lapis angularis*. On *R*. a rock, *Regnum iudaicum*.

Inscriptions: (*a*) in margin: Daniel: and Daniele ii cap°.
          (*b*) in border:

Cernit per visum daniel de rupe recisum
Absque manu lapidem: deus est et non lapis idem.

5. Top *R*. The Burning Bush. Moses, horned, on *L*., stands with his *R*. foot raised, and takes off his shoe: his *R*. hand is raised. On *R*. a green bush with flames, *Rubus*. On it a disc, with the head of Christ cross-nimbed.

Inscriptions: (*a*) in margin : Moyses : and : Exodo iii cap°.

   (*b*) in border :

     Misticus ille rubus non sensit in igne calorem
     Sic non amisit pariendo maria pudorem.

 6. Bottom *R.* Aaron's rod. A turreted arch on *L.*: under it a green altar, behind which is a green leaved tree, *virga aaron.* On *R.* is Moses pointing : three Jews behind him, surprised.

Inscriptions: (*a*) in margin : Numeri xvij cap°.

   (*b*) in border :

     Virga nucem fert uirgo ducem natura superna (? stupescit)
     In ierico fructu deico crucis uua rubescit.

 7. Bottom *L.* Two prophets (Balaam and Daniel), one with scroll points up : the other points up and down, and looks back to *L.*

Inscriptions: (*a*) in margin : Numerorum xxiiii c°. Daniele ix cap°.

   (*b*) in border :

    Balaam. Orietur stella ex iacob et exurgit homo de israel.
    Daniel. Cum uenerit sanctus sanctorum cessabit unctio uestra.

IV. f. 3 *b.*

Virtue. Nameless : throned and crowned as usual, holds a white branch of some kind.

Commandment. Non assumes nomen dei in uanum.

 1. *Centre.* The Presentation. On *L.* Joseph with doves : the Virgin holding Christ, who has a round object in his hand. The altar, with two candles. On *R.* Simeon with red nimbus, behind the altar, stretches out his hand : behind him is Anna : green steps lead up to the altar.

 In the border :

    Offert allatum symeon de uirgine natum
    Quem sic uenturum precinit (*l.* presciuit) et hunc moriturum.

 2, 3. Half-circles : two bearded prophets seated look at the central picture.

 4. Top *L.* Abraham and Melchizedek : *L.*, Abraham, in mail, with sword, holds in his arms a cloth full of loaves. *R.*, Melchizedek, in blue and red, with a cleft white mitre, holds up a quadripartite cake (or Host), his hands covered with his robe, and a chalice.

 In margin : Genesis xiiij c°.

 In border : Abraham. Melchisedech.

    Te signat christe panis quem contulit iste
    Sic quod in ede patris fieres oblacio matris.

 5. Top *R.* Dedication of Samuel. An awning on *L.* fastened to the border and twining round it : an altar : on *R.* Samuel, a child, is touching it : he is brought by Eli, bearded, behind whom are Elkanah, Hannah, and ? Peninnah.

 In margin : Reg. ...

 In border : Samuel. Ely.

    Regis in exemplo miles datur hostia templo
    Rex puer emanuel tiro puer samuel.

 E. MSS.

6. Bottom *R.* Abel's offering. Abel, bearded, with long straight hair, in blue and yellow, holds a lamb in his arms: a white draped altar: on *R.* Cain, beardless, with curling hair, in green and pink, holds a sheaf in his arms.

In margin: Genes. iiij c⁰.

In border: Abel. Cayn.

> Agnus abel munus agnus (agnum) prius optulit unus
> Offertur magnus non a populo deus agnus.

7. Bottom *L.* Two prophets (Malachi and Amos).

In margin: Malachias iii cap⁰. Amos vii c⁰.

In border:

> Malachias. Veniet ad templum suum dominator quem uos queritis.
> Amos. Vidi dominum stantem super altare.

V. f. 4 *a.*

Virtue. Humilitas, crowned, with veil, her *L.* hand raised.

Commandment. Sabbatum sanctifices.

1. *Centre.* Baptism of Christ. Christ in the centre, with red and white cross-nimbus, up to his middle in the water, which rises into a heap, and is inscribed *flumen iordanis.* The Dove comes from above on *R.* On *L.* is John Baptist with his hands out, saying: *tu uenis ad me?* On *R.* an angel holds a long red robe.

In border:

> Baptizat regem miles, noua gracia legem
> Et mundo noua lex · noua lux · nouus intonuit rex.

2. Top *L.* Crossing the Red Sea. On *L.* Moses, with short staff and hand raised, in purple and green. On *R.* a chariot, with horse falling forward to *L.*: in it are four men, two of them supplicating: a third, crowned, is Pharaoh; the fourth, armed with pennoned spear: below, dark brown sea with two heads in it.

In margin: Exodo xiiii c⁰.

In border: Moyses. Pharao.

> Vlcio digna, rei moyses baptismus hebrei
> Merguntur minat intingitur eripiuntur.

3. Top *R.* Zipporah circumcises her child. In the centre Zipporah with white nimbus, a flint in her *L.* hand, the child with red nimbus in her *R.* She holds it over a table with green cloth. Moses on *R.* faces *L.* and holds a white object in his *R.* hand and points to *L.*

In margin: Exodo iiii c⁰.

In border:

> Processit lauacrum sacra circumcisio sacrum
> Et quos castrauit petra fontis gracia lauit.

4, 5. Half-circles: two seated figures in caps, pointing upwards.

6. Bottom *R.* Noah in the ark. The ark, a church-like building in a boat, has a round window in the lower stage, and two two-light windows above. Noah at a door on *R.* sends out the dove. The dove returns from *R.* border, with a leaf in its mouth. At the bottom on *R.*, outside the medallion, the raven flies downwards with something white in its beak.

In margin : Genesis viii cap⁰.
In border :

> Archa columba noe uindex aqua coruus oliua
> Sunt cibus ecclesie lauacri sunt flumina uiua.

7. Bottom *L.* Two prophets (Moses and Joel) : the latter beardless.
In border:
Moyses. Circumcidite prepucium cordis uestri.

Johel. Omnis alienigena incircumcisus non intrabit sanctuarium meum.

VI. f. 4 *b.*

Virtue. Pacientia, holds a vase to her breast with her *R.* hand.
Commandment. Honora patrem tuum et matrem tuam.

1. *Centre.* Christ bearing the Cross. He has a purple robe round his loins, and bears the green cross to *R.* On *R.* two men, one in cap or helmet, with hammer, drags him by the hand ; the other strikes him with stick and hand. Behind Christ follow the Virgin and another woman.
In border :

> Cristus preclaram passurus fert crucis aram
> Vere coronatus consputus conuiciatus.

2. Top *L.* Elijah and the widow-woman. Elijah, bearded and bareheaded, talks to the widow, who holds two long sticks crossed saltire-wise.
In margin : Regum x. c⁰.
In border :

> Misterio digna crucis en duo colligo ligna
> Crux geminos munit populos, crux saluat et unit.

3. Top *R.* Isaac bearing the wood. He is on *L.* with a faggot on his shoulders. Abraham bears a long sword, point upwards, points to *R.*, and looks back.
In margin : Genes. xxii c⁰.
In border: Ysaac. Abraham.

> Ligna puer gerens (*l.* gestat) crucis unde typum manifestat
> Qui (? Quam) portauit ita spes mundi ueraque uita.

4, 5. Half-circles : seated men facing the centre.

6. Bottom *R.* Ezekiel's Vision of the men marked in their foreheads. On *L.* a mailed man kills a kneeling one : the heads of two more are seen. In the centre a man with his hands out, facing *R.*, is marked in the forehead with a pen by a man in white : behind, a smaller figure with raised hands faces *L.*
In margin : Ezech. ix ca.
In border :

> A nece saluantur soli taiique tuantur (? notantur)
> Vt liquet hoc signo uirtus talis est data ligno.

7. Bottom *L.* Two prophets (Isaiah and Jeremiah) with scroll and book.
In margin : Ysayas l. c⁰ sentencia m(odo) et non de uerbo ad uerbum
(i.e. the sense of the passage only is quoted).
Jeremias xi. c⁰.
In border :
Ysaias. Sicut ouis ad occisionem ductus est.

Jeremie. Dabit percucienti maxillam saturabitur obprobriis.

VII. f. 5 a.

Virtue.   Obediencia, hands in lap.
Commandment.   Non occides.

1. *Centre.*   The Crucifixion.   On *L.* of the cross stands the Church, a nimbed female holding a chalice: on *R.* a six-winged seraph sheathes his sword[1].   Above the cross-beam are two heads : the one on *L.*, beardless, looks at Christ: on *R.* is the blind-fold head of the Synagogue looking away, with arm extended to *R.*

In border :

> Nos deus exemit fusoque cruore redemit
> Morte minus digna moriens a morte maligna.

2, 3.   Half-circles : seated figures, one on a rock, the other on a throne.

4.   Top *L.*   Sacrifice of Isaac.   On *L.* the ram in the bush : above it an angel, half-length, in blue, catches the sword and hand of Abraham, in blue and green, who with his other hand holds the hair of Isaac, kneeling, with bound hands, on a green altar.

In margin : Genesis xxii c°.
In border : Abraham.

> Quem peperit sara pater offert in crucis ara
> Veruex mactatur puer incolumis reuocatur.

5.   Top *R.*   The Brazen Serpent.   Moses, horned, with the tables : in light green and blue.   The serpent on a column in the centre, horned and winged, with a wolf-like head.   Three beardless figures on the *R.*, with hands raised towards *L.*

In margin : Ioh. iii. cap°.
In border :

> Moyses.   Serpens serpentes, christus necat ignipotentes.
> Serpentes.

6.   Bottom *R.*   The Widow's Son.   A youth in bed, núde, under a green coverlet : his head, on pillow, to *L.*   Elijah bends over him, with hands raised.   The mother, with veil, and one hand outstretched, stands at the foot.

In margin : Reg. iiii. cap°.
In border : Elyas.   Sareptena.

> In cruce uita deus nos suscitat, hunc elyseus.
> Sic monstratura preco fuit ante figura.

7.   Bottom *L.*   Two prophets (Jacob and Nahum) converse.

In margin : Genesis xlix. c°.   Naum p° c°.
In border :

> Jacob.   Lauabit uino stolam suam.
> Naum.   Sepulcrum tuum quia inhonorant (*l.* inhonoratus es).

VIII. f. 5 b.

Virtue.   Nameless, supports the central medallion.
Commandment.   Non mecaberis.

1.   *Centre.*   The angel at the tomb.   He holds a palm, looks *R.*, and points down : there is the appearance of a beard on his face.   In the tomb is a cloth : on *L.* the three

---

[1] This detail of the seraph occurs in a xiiith century window of types at Sens Cathedral, N. choir aisle.

women with caskets. Under arches in the lower part of the tomb are three mailed guards sleeping : one has a sword and one a shield.

In border :

> Quod deus exiuit deus et post funera uiuit.
> Plena sacramento res est clauis monumento.

2, 3. Half-circles : two figures, one kneels with book, and the other sits.

4. Top *L.* Jonah vomited up. In front is the fish, with prominent scales, vomiting up Jonah, in blue, who clings to the trunk of a tree growing on land on *R.* Behind is Nineveh, a church inside a wall, with trefoil-headed door and lancet windows.

In margin : Jonas ii. cap°.

In border :

> Jonas. Pro ut (? Proditur ut) saluus quem ceti clauserat aluus
> Ordine sis (*l.* sic) pulcro surrexit uita sepulcro.

5. Top *R.* The lion and its young. The lion, tail in air, roaring, stands on or over a lion lying on its back : he faces *R.*

In border :

> Reddit per flatum catulum leo uiuificatum.

6. Bottom *R.* Samson in Gaza. An octagonal city containing three towers : four armed men round it with raised weapons.

In margin : Judic. xvi. c°.

In margin :

> Sampson de gaza conclusus ab hostibus exit.
> Surget de tumulo petra christus quem petra texit.

7. Bottom *L.* Two prophets (Job and Jonah) with scrolls.

In margin : Job xix. c°. Jonas ii. cap°.

In border :

> Job. Et in carne mea uid(ebo) d(eum) m(eum).
> Jonas. Subleuabis de corrupcione uitam meam, do(mine) d(eus) m(eus) t.

IX. f. 6 *a.*

Virtue. Nameless : *R.* hand raised, palm outwards.

Commandment. Non furtum facies.

1. *Centre.* Harrowing of Hell. A double gate at each side, one-half of which is unhinged. Christ enters from *L.*, wounded, with long cross-staff and banner : he takes the hand of the first of five kneeling naked figures : under their feet are devils with raised claws : one has red eyes. Behind Christ is a beardless man, in green, with joined hands. In the background is a battlemented wall. Two angels over it face each other, in adoration.

In border :

> Confractis portis religato principe mortis
> Plebs electorum transfertur ad astra polorum.

2, 3. Half-circles : seated figures.

4. Top *L.* David and the bear. David is a youth in red and green, who pulls a lamb out of the mouth of a bear running to *R.*

In margin : Reg. xvij. c°.

In border :

> Dauid.   Vrsus ouem portat dauid necat atque reportat
> Sic homo saluatur per christum morsque necatur.

5. Top *R*. Samson and the lion. He faces *L*., is bearded, in red and green, rends the lion, which moves to *L*.

In margin : Judic. xiiij. c°.

In border :

> Sampson.   Virtus sampsonis uicit strauitque leonem
> Christus tartareum uictum uincitque draconem.

6. Bottom *R*. Samson and the gates. He is beardless, and faces *L*. : gates on shoulder. A towered city on *R*. : a man in green in the gate points to him.

In margin : Judic. xvj. c°.

In border :

> Sampson.   Ablatis portis sampson gazam spoliauit
> Infernum spolians christus celum penetrauit.

7. Bottom *L*. Prophet Hosea, and Sibyl with book, pointing up.

In margin : Osee xiii. c°.

In border :

> Osee.   Ero mors tua o mors morsus tuus ero inferne.
> Sibilia.   Inquirens tetri portas infringet auerni.

X. f. 6 *b*.

Virtue.   Nameless, both hands raised.

Commandment.   Non loqueris falsum testimonium.

1. *Centre*. Ascension. Christ in the midst, arms out, full-face : clouds surround his arms : four apostles kneel on *R*., facing *L*. : the Virgin and four more kneel on *L*., facing *R*.

In border :

> Deuicta morte christus baratrique cohorte
> Ethram concendit promissaque dona rependit.

2, 3. Half-circles : kneeling figures.

4. Top *L*. Enoch translated. He has yellow robe and bluish-green nimbus : his arms out ; clouds surround his arms and chest.

In margin : Gen. v. c°.

In border :

> Enoc.   Christum signauit qui celsa poli penetrauit.
> Enoc translatus saciat quiete locatus.

5. Top *R*. Elijah taken up. He is in blue, in a green chariot, drawn by one white mule galloping to *R*., where is a cloud : he holds a whip, and pulls off a brown mantle, held by a small beardless Elisha on *L*.

In border : Heliseus.   Helias.

> Igneus heliam currus leuat ad theoriam.
> Clausa sacramenti christo fauet astra petenti.

6. Bottom *R*. The scape-goat. Four men face *R*., with hands joined, or point to a goat on *R*., which stands on its hind-legs eating a vine.

In margin : (twice) Leuitico xvi. c°.

In border:
> Hic caper alta petens alieno crimine fetens
> Signat tollentem scelus orbis et astra petentem.

7. Bottom *L.* Two prophets (Habakkuk and David).
In margin: Abacuc iii. c⁰.
In border:
> Abacuc. Leuatus est sol et luna stetit in ordine suo.
> Dauid rex. Ascendit deus in iubilacione et dominus in uoce tube.

XI. f. 7 *a.*
Virtue. Nameless; her hands in her lap.
Commandment. Non concupiscas domum proximi tui.

1. *Centre.* The Synagogue unveiled. She is seated on a throne, full-face, her arms extended; she holds in her *R.* hand the Tables of the Law, which are partly green, and seem to be sprouting: in her *L.* is a gold vase. A hand from above draws a veil off her face and head. A bearded figure stands on each side, and points to her.
In border:
> Hactenus obscuris legis uelata figuris[1]
> Adueniente fide rem synagoga uide.

2, 3. Half-circles: seated men, one cross-legged.

4. Top *L.* Ezekiel's Vision of the Wheels. He faces *R.* with raised hands. In air on *R.* are a pair of green wings, and over them a pair of wheels with eight spokes.
In margin: Ezech. p⁰ c⁰.
In border:
> Cristus in celis suspenditur ezechielis
> Cum diuinarum cernit secreta rotarum.

5. Top *R.* John Baptist: he faces *L.* in a purple robe, with gold nimbus, and points *L.* with his *R.* hand: in his *L.* he holds a disk with Paschal Lamb and banner on green ground.
In margin: Joh. p⁰ c⁰·
In border: Johannes Baptista.
> Vox uerbum uite precedens clamo uenite.
> Pando uiam numen tenebre cognoscite lumen.

6. Bottom *R.* Queen of Sheba. She stands, wearing a flat crown, and offers a gold cup to Solomon, who is crowned and seated with raised hand.
In margin: Reg. x.
In border: Regina. Rex salomon.
> Dona dat etherea regi regina sabea
> Scilicet ecclesia quam palleat allegoria.

7. Bottom *L.* Two prophets (Zephaniah and Malachi).
In margin: Sophonias iii⁰ c⁰.
In border:
> Melchias. (Inscription erased.)
> Sophonias. Sperabunt in nomine domini omnes reliquie israel.

---

[1] These and other of the verses in this MS. were inscribed on a retable in the Abbey Church at Bury St Edmund's. See my Essay thereon (*Camb. Ant. Soc.* 8vo. publications, 1895, p. 192).

XII. f. 7 b.

Virtue. Nameless, holds a red three-flowered rod.
Commandment. Non habebis deos alienos.

1. *Centre.* Triumph of the Church. Christ with book in *R.* hand seated in a chariot (one wheel of seven spokes is seen), with a female on his *L.* She has joined hands and wears a crown, which he touches with two fingers. The four cherubic beasts surround them.

In border:

> Vota (Voce) subarrata fidei meritisque sacrata
> Sponsa coronatur sponsoque deo sociatur.

2, 3. Half-circles: seated men.

4. Top *L.* Grace and the Law } two women with covered heads talking.
            Mercy and Truth }

In border:

> Virtus uirtuti fit sancta salusque saluti
> Gracia cum legi datur obuia sponsaque regi.

5. Top *R.* Righteousness and Peace: two crowned women kissing.

In border:

> Justicia et pax osculate sunt.
> (In a late hand) Justice and peace do kis together.

6. Bottom *R.* Judah and Edom. Two females support a cross with nearly equal arms. At the intersection is a disk with the bust of Christ on a blue ground, cross-nimbed.

In border:

> Hinc se iudea christo legit hinc ydumea
> Vt fiat domino grex unus de grege bino.

7. Bottom *L.* Two prophets (Zechariah and Solomon).

In margin: Zacharias iiij cap°. Salomon canticum vi. cap.

In border:

> Zacharias. Et educet lapidem primarium et exequabit gratia gratia (*l.* gratiam gratie) eius.
> Salomon. Anima mea turbata est propter quadrigas aminadab.

II. Apocalypse, illustrated: with explanations in Norman-French. Cent. xiii. The illustrations occupy two-thirds of the page: the ground is uncoloured. The frames are alternately of blue and light red with gold corners. This Apocalypse resembles very closely a copy in the Lambeth Library (no. 434) with 90 pictures and text in French. The Lambeth MS. has at the beginning

Iste liber est de co*mmun*itate sororum de ....d. P. 18.

I subjoin a list of the pictures in the Eton MS.:

1. John preaches to the people. So in the Lambeth MS.
2. Baptizes Drusiana. So in the Lambeth MS.

3. Before Domitian. ⎫
4. Sent to sea.   ⎬ These two pictures gone in Lambeth MS.
5. Before Domitian again.
6. In the cauldron. After this 2 ff. are gone in the Lambeth MS.
7. Sent to sea again.
8. At Patmos: an angel appears.
9. Sees the seven angels in churches.
10. At the feet of Christ, who has key and sword and golden feet.
11. With the angel: door opened in heaven. Follows no. 6 in the Lambeth MS.
12. Christ in gold mandorla: the beasts: the Elders: the seven lamps.
13. God on the throne: the book: the Lamb: John, Elder, and Angel.
14. The Lamb opens the book: the Lamb on Sion adored by angels and Elders.
15. John: the first beast (Angel) speaks from clouds: man on white horse with bow.
16. John: the second beast (Calf) speaks from clouds: man on red horse with sword.
17. John: the third beast (Lion) speaks from clouds: man on black horse with scales.
18. John: the fourth beast (Eagle) speaks from clouds: man on pale horse: fire in hand: Hell-mouth follows.
19. John: souls under altar, clothed by two angels.
20. John: sun, moon, stars, rocks fall: kings flee.
21. John: angels on corners of quatrefoil (Earth) hold winds (human heads): angel under the sun speaks.
22. John: speaks to Elder with crown and scroll.
23. God on throne: the Lamb: beasts, Elders, and multitude adore.
24. Angel gives trumpets to four others.
25. Angel with censer before altar: Christ in air over it: three angels with trumpets behind.
26. John: angel empties censer of fire into earth: thunders (represented by human faces) and lightnings in sky.
27. John: first trumpet: hail and fire.
28. John: second trumpet: mountains of fire in the sea: a ship.
29. John: third trumpet: a black star falls: men drinking.
30. John: fourth trumpet: a third of the sun dark: moon and stars fall.
31. John: fourth trumpet: an eagle flying with scroll *ve ve ve habitantibus in terra.*
32. John: fifth trumpet: star with key opens pit: locusts and warriors come out.
33. John: sixth trumpet: angel speaks from altar: four angels armed stand in the waters of *Eufraten.*
34. Three horsemen: fire comes from the horses' mouths: they attack seated people.
35. John stops his ears: seventh trumpet sounded.
36. Adoration of God by Elders and angels.
37. John writes: angel in air forbids him: seven thunders (faces vomiting fire) in air.
38. Angel with foot on sea and foot on land gives book to John, who is bearded.
39. Two bearded witnesses hold a scroll: *Dominus ihc xpc interficiet te spiritu oris sui:* they stand before a seated man, who draws a sword.

This picture is no. 29 in the Lambeth MS.: the same inscription on the scroll: Antichrist has a hare-headed devil at his ear.

40. Two men with swords: one beheads a kneeling man: beardless figure lies on his back: angel carries up two souls.

41. Michael and two angels fight two dragons (one is small).

42. John: dragon coiled up: angel with palm speaks from heaven.

43. John: dragon coiled up, casts out water: angel gives wings to crowned female, who flies to *R.*

44. Four saints fight the dragon.

45. John. Temple of God opened in heaven: below are thunders and hail.

46. Woman crowned with stars hands child to angel in air. Dragon on *L.*

47. John: beast comes out of the sea.

48. Dragon greets the beast of the sea.

49. John: men worship the beast.

50. The beast blasphemes, open-mouthed: John sits on *R.*: over him is Christ, half-length.

51. The beast in centre: saints on each side fighting it, and slain by it.

52. John: beast like a lamb comes out of the earth.

53. The lamb-like beast touches a king with its fore-leg: men adore the seven-headed beast: fire falls out of heaven.

54. A man with sword presides over tables of various foods and wines, on which stands the lamb-like beast: on *L.* five people point to their foreheads.

55. Two soldiers slay two men: the lamb-like beast on his hind legs makes four men adore the beast standing on an altar. John on *R.*

56. John: the Lamb on Sion: people stand below and worship.

57. The new song.   1—4.   Four beasts.
            5.   Christ.
       6, 8.   Angels with harps.
       7, 9.   Elders.
         10.   Worshippers.

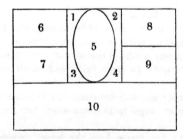

58. John: angel flies through heaven: men sit below.

59. John: second angel: Babylon fallen: heads seen in the ruins.

60. John: third angel: devil pulls souls into Hell-mouth with rope: beast on altar supported by columns.

61. John at desk: angel in sky (*Beati mortui*): dead people lie round: their souls received in a cloth by an angel.

62. John: crowned man in a cloud, with sickle: angel speaks out of temple in air. Below, crowned man reaping.

63. Angel hands a book out of temple: angel below cuts vine: green juice reaching to the necks of two horses on *R.*: under arches, on *L.* of which, facing them, is a devil with club. Angel above speaks from under altar with chalice on it.

64. John: five angels on cloud with vials.

65. John: six angels with harps.

66. John: one of the four beasts (the Lion) in long robe with lion's paws, head, and feet, gives gold vials to seven angels: temple behind.

67. John: first Vial emptied on prostrate men.

68. John (on *R.* seated): second Vial emptied on sea: dead men in it.

69. John: third Vial emptied on river.

70. Angel and John: Christ in mandorla: fourth angel with vial on *R.*

71. Fourth Vial poured on the sun, which emits red flames: three men sit with hands to foreheads.

72. Fifth Vial poured on vacant seat of beast: six men sit gnawing their tongues.

73. John: sixth Vial poured on Euphrates, which flows on one side.

74. John bearded: the lamb-like beast (false prophet) and two seven-headed beasts: a frog comes from the mouth of each.

75. Seventh Vial: angel speaks from heaven: hail falls: fallen city and heads in it, below.

76. John and angel: scarlet woman sits on eight blue streams, and holds a round object: she has gold diadem and veil.

77. John on angel's back: woman in brown with gold cup on seven-headed beast.

78. John: angel speaks from heaven: ruins of Babylon full of demons.

79. Angel with millstone on shoulder: millstone in sea: city behind.

80. John seated: three angels blow trumpets in heaven: woman lying on her back in flames in Hell-mouth, a cup in her hand.

81. Christ in mandorla: four beasts: elders below.

82. John: angel with trumpet in heaven: a table: the Lamb upon it puts his foot on the ring of his seated Bride: five guests, two on *R.*, three on *L.*

83. John seated: angel with scroll: Christ in sky half-length: John kneels to angel, who points to Christ.

84. John seated: horsemen in air; the foremost on a white horse, sword in mouth, cusped nimbus, blood on his vesture: Christ below on earth, with sword, half-length.

85. John: angel stands in air: birds fly down to pick the eyes of prostrate kings and men.

86. John seated: Christ on white horse, cusped nimbus, sword, rides down from heaven to fight three kings on a seven-headed beast.

87. Christ comes from *L.* on horse: two mailed men with pronged sticks thrust beast into lake.

88. John: angel comes from heaven with key and chain: another angel binds the dragon with a rope.

89. Angel leads dragon with chain and key: on *R.*, he locks the abyss over the bound dragon.

90. Three bearded men on a throne: naked souls on each side. So also in Lambeth 434.

91. Soldiers behind the head of the dragon emerging from the pit: two archers and a horseman on *R.* attack a walled city with four praying men on the walls.

92. Hell-mouth, containing men, dragon, and two beasts.

93. John: below him six naked souls emerge from the sea. Christ in mandorla holds up two books: on *R.* naked souls on land.

94. John with pen: angel speaks from heaven: below, a richly ornamented laver, which John is going to measure.

95. Angel and John: the new Jerusalem shewn in a ground-plan: the Lamb in the midst of it on gold ground: the names of the twelve gems are marked. The same design in Lambeth 434.

96. John seated: men adore the mandorla, in which are the Father and the Lamb: a triple river flows from it, between two trees. The same arrangement in Lambeth 434.

97. John kneels to the angel, who raises him and points to Christ in mandorla.

98. John with scroll (inscribed later FINIS · AN · ENDE ·) kneels to Christ, nimbed and throned, beardless, holding apparently an inverted taper.

178.

ANTHEM BOOK.

Vellum, 23¼ × 17, ff. 125. Cent. xvi. (1500–1510).

In the original boards, covered with stamped leather with Tudor badges.

The covers are lined with four sheets (eight leaves) of a fine copy of the Epistles of cent. xi., xii., measuring about 12 × 9 inches, in double columns of 51 lines each: they contain parts of 1, 2 Cor., Gal., Eph. There is a stichometric note at the end of 1 Cor.

Expl. EPLA · I · AD · CORINTH' · HAB̄ · VERS̄ · DCCC · LXX ·

Collation : a⁸ (wants 8) b⁸ (wants 3–6) c⁸ (wants 4, 5) d⁸ e gone f⁸ (wants 1, 2, 7, 8) g⁸–m⁸ n o p gone q⁸ r⁸ (wants 4, 5) s gone t⁸ (wants 1–3, 6, 7) v⁸ x⁸ y gone z⁸ aa gone bb⁸ (wants 2–7) cc dd gone ee⁸⁺¹ (wants 4–6): 99 leaves are gone.

The book was evidently written for the College Chapel: the arms of the College are in the first initial. The initials throughout are remarkable: some contain shields, and a few, figures. There are two styles of initial, one being the ordinary style of the illu-mination of the period, with fluid gold and natural flowers, very carefully done, and of a foreign aspect; the other style is that of the ornamental penman.

I have noted the following initials:

1. f. 1 *b.* Arms of Eton College.
2. ff. 33 *b*, 34 *a.* Initials to a *Salue Regina* in nine parts: the initials shew nine

choirs of angels with scrolls, on which the names of the nine orders are written: the angels do not differ in form or attributes from each other: they are thus distributed:

f. 33 b.	f. 34 a.
Seraphyn, Quatriplex.	Troni, Medius.
Cherubyn, Triplex.	Principatus, Secundus contratenor.
Dominationes, Primus contratenor.	Virtutes, Inferior contratenor.
Potestates, Tenor.	Archangeli, Secundus bassus.
Angeli, Primus bassus.	

On the lower margin of f. 34 a are these lines, which explain how the music was to be sung:

> Antiphona hec christi laudem sonat atque marie
>   Et decus angelicis concinit ordinibus
> Qui sunt angeli erunt archangeli et ordo sequetur
> Virtutum—que potestatum, tunc principat alter
> Post domina-que-tiones adde tronos cherubynque
> Et seraphyn junges qui loca summa tenent.

3. f. 36 b. In an initial are the words Robertus Wylkynson cuius anime propicietur deus.

4. ff. 64 b, 65 a. Four shields in the initials to an anthem by Davy, *O domine celi terreque.*

    (*a*) Arms of England.
    (*b*) Arms of the Confessor.
    (*c*) Arms of Magdalen College, Oxford.
    (*d*) Sable a fess *or* between three stags' heads couped *argent*, two and one.

At the end of the anthem is:

hanc antiphonam composuit Ricardus Davy uno die collegio Magdalene Oxoniis.

5. f. 47 b. A large initial, gold ground, to an anthem by W. Lambe. S. John Baptist, with scroll *ecce agnus dei:* a lamb on a book by him.

6. f. 50 a. Arms of Eton College.

The stave is of 5 lines.

There are two remarkable indices to the book, one at each end; the second is an incomplete replica of the first, which I here transcribe:

Name of the Antiphon	Number of parts: in red	Composer's name	Quire: in red	Leaf of quire	?: in red
Aue lumen gracie	4 parcium	ffayrefax	t	5	14
Ad te purissima uirgo	5 pc	Cornysch	s	7	22
Ascendit cristus	4 pc	Lambe	v	6	14
Aue cuius concepcio	4 pc	ffayrefax	o	3	22
Aue maria mater dei	5 pc	Cornysch	x	4	15
Aue lux tocius mundi	5 pc	Browne	p	2	21
Ascendit cristus	5 pc	Huchynge	z	5	21

Name of the Antiphon	Number of parts: in red	Composer's name	Quire: in red	Leaf of quire	?: in red
Gaude flore uirginali (1)	7 pc	Kellyk	a	5	23
(2)	6 pc	Davy	b	6	22
(3)	6 pc	Wylkynson	c	4	22
(4)	6 pc	Cornysch	f	2	23
(5)	5 pc	Dunstable	o	8	21
(6)	5 pc	Turges	r	1	22
(7)	4 pc	Turges	x	2	14
(8)	5 pc	Lambe	n	5	21
(9)	5 pc	Horwud	m	5	21
(10)	5 pc	Browne	p	5	22
(11)	4 pc	Lambe	v	8	14
Gaude uirgo mater christi (1)	6 pc	Sturton	d	6	15
(2)	5 pc	Horwud	m	8	21
(3)	4 pc	Wylkynson	t	8	14
(4)	4 pcium	Cornysch	x	5	14
Gaude rosa sine spina	5 pc	Hawkynes	q	6	22
Gaude uirgo salutata (1)	4 pc	Holy < n > gborne	x	7	19
(2)	5 pcium	Hawkynes	q	4	22
In honore summe matris	5 pcium	Davye	l	8	22
Nesciens mater uirgo uirum	5 pcium	Lambe	r	3	22
O domine celi terreque	5 pc	Davye	k	4	22
O maria saluatoris mater	8 pc	Browne	a	1	22
O maria plena gracia	6 pc	Lambe	b	1	21
O Regina celestis glorie (1)	6 pc	Lambe	c	4	23
(2)	5 pc	Lambe	n	2	20
O Regina mundi clara	6 pc	Browne	d	3	15
O Maria et Elizabeth	5 pc	Banester	m	3	21
O mater uenerabilis	5 pc	Browne	r	7	18
Virgo prudentissima	6 pc	Wylkynson	c	1	22
Virgo uirginum preclara	4 pc	Lambe	f	7	14
Quid cantemus innocentes	5 pc	ffayrefax	o	5	21
Salue regina uas mundicie	6 pc	Hawkynes	e	7	23
Salue decus castitatis	5 pc	Wylkynson	r	4	22
Salue Ihesu mater uera	5 pc	Davye	w	7	22
Salue Regina (1)	7 pc	Sutton	h	4	23
(2)	5 pc	Horwud	g	2	21
(3)	5 pc	Davye	g	4	23
(4)	5 pc	Cornysch	g	6	22
(5)	5 pc	Lambe	h	2	22
(6)	5 pc	Browne	g	8	21
(7)	5 pc	Browne	i	8	15
(8)	5 pc	Hacumplaynt	h	6	22
(9)	5 pc	Hygons	i	6	22
(10)	5 pc	Huchyne	h	8	22
(11)	5 pc	Hampton	k	2	22
(12)	5 pc	Wylkynson	l	2	22

Name of the Antiphon		Number of parts: in red	Composer's name	Quire: in red	Leaf of quire	?: in red
Salue Regina (13)		5 pc	ffayrefax	i	4	22
(14)		5 pc	Brygeman	f	7	19
Stabat mater dolorosa	(1)	6 pc	Browne	c	1	22
	(2)	5 pc	ffayrefax	o	1	21
A marginal note here : *bonus cantus* (3)		5 pc	Cornysch	q	1	23
	(4)	5 pc	Cornysch	p	7	18
	(5)	5 pc	Davye	l	2	21
Stabat iuxta christi crucem		6 pc	Browne	d	1	14
Stabat uirgo mater christi (1)		6 pc	Browne	c	6	23
(2)		4 pc	Browne	v	2	14
Stella celi		4 pc	Lambe	r	4	15
Virgo templum trinitatis		5 pc	Davy	l	5	22
Virgo gaude gloriosa		5 pc	Lambe	n	7	21
Et exultauit (1)		7 pc	Browne	y	2	22
(2)		5 pc	Nesbett	y	8	22
(3)		5 pc	Davye	y	5	22
(4)		5 pc	Kellyk	z	4	22
(5)		5 pc	Horwud	z	2	23
(6)		5 pc	ffayrefax	aa	3	22
(7)		5 pc	Lambe	z	7	21
(8)		5 pc	Cornysch	bb	3	23
(9)		5 pc	Browne	aa	1	22
(10)		5 pc	Browne	bb	5	22
(11)		6 pc	Wylkynson	bb	1	22
(12)		5 pc	Wylkynson	aa	7	22
(13)		5 pc	Mychelson	aa	8	22
(14)		5 pc	Brygeman	aa	5	19
(15)		blank				
(16)		4 pc	Sygar	bb	8	21
(17)		4 pc	Browne	cc	2	22
(18)		4 pc	Turges	cc	4	21
(19)		4 pc	Turges	cc	6	17
(20)		4 pc	Baldwyn	cc	8	22
(21)		4 pc	Baldwyn	dd	4	22
(22)		4 pc	Sygar	dd	2	22
(23)		blank				
(24)		blank				
(25)		4 pc	Turges	dd	6	14
(26)		4 pc	Stratford	cc	2	14
(27)		5 pc	Davye	dd	8	14
(28)		blank				
Dominica in Ramis palmarum. Passio domini		4 pc	Davy	cc	4	22

One of the anthems has the word *regali* written by it.

On the verso of the last leaf is the Creed set to music and

divided among the Twelve Apostles, by Robertus Wylkynson. The following couplet is written below it:

> huius distinctas muse tot sumite partes
> margine quot paruo nomina scripta uides.

The second index goes down to Virgo templum trinitatis.

I add the Christian names of the composers as they appear in various parts of the book, at the beginnings of the several compositions.

1. Willelmus Horwud.
2. Ricardus Davy.
3. Willelmus Cornysch.
4. Johannes Browne.
5. Walterus Lambe.
6. Johannes Sutton (p. 50 a: Eton arms in the initial).
7. Nicholaus Howchyn.
8. Robertus Feyrfax.
9. Ricardus Hygons.
10. Johannes Hampton.
11. Gilbertus Banester.
12. Edmundus Turges.
13. Hugo Kellyk.
14. Robertus ⎫
15. Johannes ⎭ Wylkynson.

Of these names nos. 2, 3, 4, 8, 11, and probably others, are well known to musicians: they occur in a MS. once belonging to Ralph Thoresby of Leeds (*Cat. MSS. Angl.* ii. p. 229, no. 7573).

Similar MSS. exist at Caius College, Cambridge, and Lambeth Palace.

Compositions by some of these authors are printed in Stafford Smith's *Musica Antiqua*.

179.

Biblia Sacra.

Uterine vellum, 6 × 4, ff. 542, in double columns. Cent. xiii., xiv. In a minute hand, Anglo-Norman. In an English binding of cent. xvii.

Contents :

The following points in the order and contents of the volume are worth noting:

Esdras i = Ezra.
Neemias ii = Nehemiah.
Esdras iii = 4 (or 2) Esdras i, ii, often called 5 Esdras, part 1.

It is divided into chapters as follows:

c. i.	Liber esdre prophete,	i. 1 of our chapters.
ii.	Quid tibi faciam iacob,	i. 24 ,,
iii.	Hec dicit deus, Ego eduxi,	ii. 1 ,,
iiii.	Hec dicit deus ad esdram,	ii. 10 ,,
v.	Ego esdras accepi,	ii. 33 ,,

Esdras iiii = 3 (or 1) Esdras.
Esdras v = 4 (or 2) Esdras ii.–xiv.
Esdras vi = 4 (or 2) Esdras xv., xvi., or 5 Esdras, part 2.

The MS. is not included in the late Professor Bensly's list of English MSS. containing 4 Esdras.

The Psalter is followed by two prologues, (a) *Cum omnes prophetas*, (b) *Dauid filius Iesse*, and by orationes, secreta, commemorations and post-communions.

The running-titles of Wisdom and Ecclesiasticus are interchanged. In the New Testament the Acts follow the Catholic Epistles.

The *Interpretationes Nominum* begin on f. 518.

The following figured initials occur:

1. *Genesis.* An I divided into six trefoil-headed compartments with blue grounds.
   (1) Christ holds a scroll inscribed *fiat*, and a globe marked *Asia*, *Africa*, *Europa*, and surrounded by CELVM.
   (2) Christ with scroll, *fiat firmamentum*.
   (3) ,, *germinet terra herb.*
   (4) ,, *fiant luminaria.*
   (5) ,, *producant aque reptil.* : birds and fish on *R.*
   (6) ,, man, woman and beasts on *R.*
   1 *Regum.* A good decorative initial.
2. *Psalterium. Beatus uir.* David sits cross-legged, playing his harp.
3. *Parabolae.* Solomon holding a scroll.
   Mattheus. A good decorative initial with dragon.
4. *ad Romanos.* Paul seated, writing.

On the fly-leaf at the end is a faint note of cent. xv.:

Ista biblia sunt (or sac...) magistri canapede doctore quem emebat apud hereford pro iii^li vi^s iiij^d.

E. MSS. 8

At the beginning:

Jo. Walter 1625; and an erased note.

Also:

Liber collegii B. M. de Etona d. d. Edw. Betham Socius 1776.

By the book-plate is pencilled:

"Time of Henry 3rd, Saml Meyrick LL.D."

180.

GREEK PRAYER-BOOK.

Paper, 5¾ × 3¾.   Cent. xvii.
There is no cover: the MS. was brought from Mount Athos.

Inc. ἀρχὴ τῶν ἑορτῶν δεσποτικοῦ μαρτήρων ἀρχαγγύλων ἀναργίρων...

181.

HORAE.

Vellum, 6⅜ × 4½, ff. 140.   Cent. xv. (1470 ?).
Bound in red leather.   The following owners' names occur:

E libris Ant. Storer.
Donum Frederici comitis Carliolensis an. Dom. 1776.

Contents:

Kalendar in French, in black and red . . . . f.	1
Sequentiae of the Gospels	13
Hours of the Cross	18
Hours of the Holy Ghost	22
Hours of the Virgin	25
Seven Psalms and Litany	69
Officium Mortuorum	85
Obsecro te	126 b
O intemerata	130 b
Stabat Mater	132 b
Quand on se veult confesser	134 b
Memoriae (of SS. Sebastian, Nicolas, Pantaleon, Agnes, Barbara) .	138 b

In the Kalendar:

Jan.	S. Savinian, in red.
	S. Savine.
7 Ap.	S. Winebault.
30 Ap.	S. Vordre.
27 July.	S. Loup, in red.

In the Litany:

SS. Savinian and Quintin, *Martyrs:* Frodobert, Aventinus, Lupus, *Confessors:* Savina, Mastidia, Syria, *Virgins.*

All of these except Quintin are Troyes saints.

The MS. is undoubtedly of the diocese of Troyes. The use is that of Sens.

The following miniatures, of fair style, occur:

1. *Sequentia of S. John.* Half-page, with border of flowers and line and leaf ornament. S. John on isle, writing; on his knee a scroll. *In principio erat uerbum.* Eagle holds inkstand : town behind.

2. *Hours of the Cross.* Crucifixion : on *L.* the Virgin, S. John, and Mary Magdalene (?): on *R.* centurion and two horsemen: Jerusalem in the background.

3. *Hours of the Holy Ghost.* Descent of the Holy Ghost: the Virgin in the midst, arms extended : dove in centre of a rose-window behind, rayed : some of the Apostles kneel.

4. *Hours of the Virgin.* Annunciation: angel on *R.* kneels with sceptre ; dove on ray : architecture in gold. The other Hours have only partial borders, and initials.

5. *Seven Psalms and Litany.* David kneels, face *L.*, on a lawn outside a city gate. In air is a red angel with a sword: crown and harp on ground.

6. *Obsecro te.* Full-page. Pietà by the Cross: two angels in air ; the one on *L.* has lance, reed and sponge, and nails: that on *R.* has scourge and column.

182.

ALCHEMICAL TRACTS.

Paper, 11⅞ × 8, ff. 161 (+ 8 fly-leaves). Cent. xvi. (1573). Written in Germany.

Contents:

1. Liber de Alkimia qui bucella dulcedinis uocatur.

In 118 chapters. At the end is:

W. 1573. B
Henry Gibbon.

At the beginning is a good initial in gold and colours.

8—2

2. Speculum hominum.

Dated 1574.

3. Breuiarum Iohannis pauperis de arte Alkymia.

In seven chapters.

4. Speculum elementorum, by Joh. Vienensis : called *O uenerande pater*.
5. Tractatus mirabilis.

Occupying three pages.

6. Hermes de salibus et corporibus.

[C. M. A. 6.]

183.   Bp. 3. 7.

MÉMOIRE HISTORIQUE ET POLITIQUE SUR LA PROVINCE DE
LANGUEDOC.

Paper, 14⅜ × 9½, ff. 181.   Cent. xvii. (31 Dec. 1697).
By M. de Bâville, Conseiller d'État, Intendant.   Drawn up by
order of the Duke of Burgundy.   There are two maps and a few
drawings.
Bequeathed by Nicolas Mann in 1754.

[C. M. A. *vac.*]

184.   Bp. 3. 11.

SUPPLEMENT TO WALPOLE'S *HISTORIC DOUBTS.*

Paper, 11⅝ × 7⅝, 26 pp.   Cent. xviii.
"In Lord Orford's hand."   Presented by E. C. H(awtrey) in
1853.

[C. M. A. *vac.*]

185.   Bp. 3. 13.

JO. DAUTH DE REBUS PUBLICIS SAXONIAE.

Paper, 11¾ × 7¾, ff. 102.   Cent. xvi., xvii.

Discursus generalis et specialis de Rerumpublicarum inferioris Saxoniae illustrium perfecto regimine et statu, oppositus Guelficis male consutis centonibus, etc.

At the end is the signature

Ioannes Dauth D. Francus suâ manu.

[C. M. A. 48.]

186. Bp. 3. 14.

REGISTER OF DESPATCHES.

Paper, 13½ × 8½, ff. 400.   Cent. xvii.·(1626).

Premier Registre de depesches envoyés ez pais estrangers par Mgr. de' Herbault en l'an mil six cens vingt six.

Bequeathed by Nicolas Mann, 1754.

[C. M. A. vac.]

187. Bp. 3. 15.

HISTOIRE DE PH. DE WAURIN.

Paper, 13⅞ × 8¾, ff. 465 written.   Cent. xvii.

Suite de l'histoire d'Angleterre ecrite par Messire Philippe de Waurin.

Transcribed from a MS. in the Bibliothèque du Roi.   Waurin's history has been edited in the Rolls Series.

Bequeathed by Nicolas Mann, 1754.

[C. M. A. vac.]

188. Bp. 4. 18.

LETTERS OF SIR H. WOTTON.

Bound in a folio volume, 12 × 9.

They were written by Wotton between 1617 and 1620, when he was Ambassador at Venice : there are also letters of Gregorio di

Monte (1619, 1620), and others, with a few other state papers.   All
Wotton's letters are printed in the *Reliquiae Wottonianae*.

The volume was presented by Lord Montague in 1833.

[C. M. A. *vac.*]

189.   Bp. 5. 16.

THEODORI LIBER POENITENTIALIS.

Paper, 11¼ × 9, pp. 116.   Cent. xviii.

A transcript of the Penitential of Theodore, Abp of Canterbury, from the MS. at Corpus Christi College, Cambridge; made
by Fr. Muriall, Fellow of Corpus Christi, and collated with the
original by Dr Thomas Greene, Master.   Perhaps made for
Mr Huggett.

[C. M. A. *vac.*]

190.   Bp. 5. 18.

B. ARETINI BELLUM SACRUM.

Paper, 11½ × 8.   Cent. xvi. (1501).

Benedicti de Accoltis Aretini de bello a Christianis contra
Barbaros gesto pro Christi sepulcro ac Judea recuperandis.

The prologue (addressed to Piero de' Medici) and first leaf of
text are supplied in a later hand.

[C. M. A. 26.]

191.

CHRONICLE OF THE WORLD IN ROLL-FORM.

Vellum roll, 21 ft. 6 in. × 13¼ in.   Cent. xv. (1420).

A Chronicle of the World from the Creation to the time of
Henry V.

Coarsely written : illustrated with medallions of the following subjects :

1. Christ seated on the rainbow, in a gold-starred sky.
2. Adam and Eve at the tree: the serpent round it.
3. Noah and his family in the ark (a ship with a red house in it).
4. King Brute: three sons before him.
5. The Nativity: ox, ass, the Virgin and Joseph. Shields of kings. The Saxon kings are represented by red and blue medallions, with crowns, orbs, and sceptres. The Norman dukes bear the three lions. Constantine bears *or*, a double-headed eagle *sa.*, Arthur *az.*, three crowns *or*.
The English kings are represented by their shields.
6. Bust of S. Thomas of Canterbury with cloven head.

[C. M. A. *vac.*]

192.

ROLL OF NEW YEAR'S GIFTS.

Vellum, 13 ft. 6 in. × 15¾ in. Cent. xvi. (27 Elizabeth).
New Year's Gifts presented to Queen Elizabeth at Westminster. Signed by the Queen.

[C. M. A. *vac.*]

193.

VENETORUM NOBILIUM LIBER.

Paper, 11 × 8, ff. 90, 30 lines to a page. Cent. xvi.
Collation: A⁴–H⁴ (signatures cease) || a⁴–o⁴ p².

Contents :

Priuilegium magni Alexandri sclauis et lingue eorum concessum ex quodam libro greco antiquissimo, apud constantinopolim reperto extractum latinum de uerbo ad verbum translatum.

Nos Alexander Philippi Regis macedonum archos monarchiae figuratus . f. 1
Ends: totius orbis.

Ego Julianus Baldasar seccretarius hoc priuilegium Dalmatiae in quadam Bibliotheca antiquissima reperi. . . . . 1 *b*
Jesù mcccx a di xxvii Zugno indictione viii.
Letter from Doge Pietro Gradenigo to Zorzi Dolphin Baylo of Armenia . 1 *b*

List of the citizens of Venice who in December 1379 "se offerse alla guerra de Zenonesi de andar con le soe persone al aquisto de Chioza" 2*b*

List of the "xxx casade che romase del conseglio zoe le soprascritte": and of the "altre xxx casade che fono ballotade alincontro de le soprascritte ballotadi a do a do," etc. 7*b*

Questa si e la uera summa de tutte le xxx casade de citadini fono fatti del conseglio alla guerra di Zenonesi del mccclxxxi. 12

xii casade de tribuni piu antixi 12*b*
Nomi de casade mudade 12*b*
xv casade enrolled in 1310 13
vii casade enrolled in 1296 13
Casade enrolled in 1297 . . . . 13*b*
Caualeria of Candia 13*b*
Prologue to the list of "Zentil homini da Venetia" 15
Le nobel fameglie et casade de Venetia 17

In alphabetical order: the arms of each family neatly drawn and blazoned in colours, in the left hand margin of each page.

The Catalogue runs from

Anafesto *to*
Zustignani (f. 89).

f. 90 is blank.

No doubt given by Wotton.

[C. M. A. 122.]

Addendum (see page 5).

10. Bk. 1. 10.

R. Hampole on the Psalms.

Vellum, ff. 170, double columns of 40 lines each. Cent. xv.

Collation: a¹⁶ b¹²–h¹² i¹⁰ k¹²–o¹² = 170 leaves + 2 blank at each end.

Inc. ...gret habundance of gasteli comforth.

Expl. in ye joy of heuen. Amen.

[C. M. A. 10.]

INDEX.

Accoltis, B. de, Bellum Sacrum, **190**.
Adelardus of Bath, **161**.
Alanus, Aequivoca, **84**.
Alberti, Leo Bapt., works by, **85, 128**.
Albertus Magnus in Luc. et Marc., **44**.
Alchemy, tracts on, **182**.
Alexander de Essebie, liber festiualis, **20. 2**.
Alexander Magnus,
  Ep. ad Aristotelem, **133**.
  Life, in Greek, **163**.
  and *see* **193**.
Ambrose, S.,
  on Psalm cxviii., **5**.
  Pastorale, **21**.
  tracts, **46, 145**.
Anastasius de fide, **144**.
Anonymous,
  Scripture history, **4**.
  on the Book of Wisdom, **19. 2**.
  Sermons, **38, 41, 120**.
  notes on Scripture, **48**.
  Allegoriae, **120**.
  de Bona Fortuna, **129**.
  poem in Italian, **159**.
  tract on Physics, **160**.
  verses, **160**.
Anselm, S., tracts by, **32, 81, 120**.
Anthem Book, **178**.
Apocalypse, illustrated, **177**.
Apuleius, L.,
  Metamorphoses and Florida, **147**.
Arabic MS., **162**.
Arator, Hist. Apost., **150**.
Arden, **24**.
Aretinus, B., Bellum Sacrum, **190**.

Aristotle,
  Ethica Nicom., **122, 129**.
  Politica, **129**.
  Rhetorica, **129**.
  Poetica, **129**.
Arms, **92–95, 140, 151, 156, 164, 178, 191, 193**.
Athanasius, Pseudo-, synopsis, **144**.
Athenagoras, **100**.
Augustine, S.,
  in Psalmos, **6, 7**.
  in Joannem, **101**.
  de Civitate Dei, **107**.
  de Trinitate, **108**.
  Epistolae, **105**.
  Sermones, **105, 106**.
  Regula, **106**.
  Vita, **106**.
  Tractatus, **37, 38, 47, 48, 120**.
Aurora, Petri de Riga, **169**.
Azure, receipt for making, **43**.

Barenguidus, *see* Berengaudus.
Bartholomaeus de Pisis, Vita S. Francisci, **118**.
Batson, Gosuin, **167**.
Bâville, M. de, **183**.
Beaumont, Jos., Theological works, **49–73**.
Bedwod, H., Anatomie of Spayne, **164**.
Bembo, Bern., notes by, **128, 137, 138**.
Benvenuto da Imola, Comm. on Dante, **115**.
Berengaudus, in Apocalypsim, **24, 76**.
Bernard, S.,
  tracts by, **32, 39**.
  Homiliae, **38, 39**.

(*Bernard, S.*)
  Tractatus vi., 120.
  letter, 124.
Bible Hystorial, 3.
Biblia, 1, 2, 25–29, 179.
  Gloss. on Psalms, 9 ; xii. Proph., 23 ;
    Matthew, 43, 77.
  Psalters, 75, 78.
  Evangelia Slavonica, 40.
Biblia Pauperum, 177.
Bibliorum Figurae, 177.
Binding, 5, 119, 178.
Boccaccio, de Mul. claris, 158.
Boethius, tracts by, 120, 129.
Boxley, 173.
Bracton, H., de legibus, 176.
Burton, J., 142.

Caeretus, Franc., 151.
Campbell, Archibald, Bp, 111.
Canons, Eccl., in Greek, 121, 144.
Cantor, Petrus,
  in Gen., Ex., Lev., 14.
  in Esdr., Neem., Paral., 16.
  in Prophetas, 19.
Case, G., poem on Judges, 173.
Cassiodorius,
  Hist. tripartita, 131.
  excerpt, 47.
Catalogus Sanctorum, 99.
Cautiones, 119, 127.
Charms, 32.
Chronicle, roll, 191.
Chronicon anon., 144.
Chrysostom, Pseudo-, Opus imperfectum,
  42 ; *see* Johannes Chrysostomus.
Cicero, M. T.,
  Aratea, 88.
  Paradoxa, Laelius, Cato Maior, Timaeus,
    90.
  de officiis, 149, 190.
Clocks, planetary, treatise on, 172.
Collier, Jer., 111.
Comestor, Peter, 3.
  Historia Scholastica, 45, 125.
Composers of cent. xv., English, 178.
Councils, Ecclesiastical, 121, 144.
Cydonius, Dem., Oratio, 11.

Cypher, a, 80.
Cyriacus of Ancona, notes by, 141.
Cyrillus, Lexicon, 86.

Dante,
  Divina Commedia, 112.
  Comm. on, 115.
Dauth, J., 185.
Dechair, 100.
Decreta,
  Table on, 36.
  extracts, 83.
  complete, 97.
Dictionary, 4.
Dionysius Areopagita, S., tracts by, 120, 131.
Dionysius Periegetes, 146.
Distinctiones argute, 83.
Dondis, J. de, on clocks, 172.
Dorotheus, Pseudo-, Synopsis, 144.

Easby, Alexander of, 20. 2.
Egidius, expositio, 35.
Elizabeth, Queen, signature of, 192.
Enjedinus, G., 73.
Esdras, 4th Book of, 179.
Ethridge, G., poem on Wyatt, 148.
Eustathius,
  in Dionys. Perieg., Gr., 146.
  in Eth. Nicom., Lat., 121.
Eutropius, 155.
Evangelia Slavonica, 40.

Farfa, documents relating to, 124.
Flores Historiarum, 123.
Forda, Joh. de, 109.
Francis, S., Life of, 118.
Franciscus Cyprius, de Purgatorio, 166.
Fraternity, Letter of, 33, 170.
Fromosigine, Joh., 110.
Fulgentius, Mythologiae, 117.

Galen, 127, 132.
Gascoigne, Doctor, 108.
Gearing, Simon, 167.
Gelasius Cyzicenus, 144.
Gentry of England and Wales, List of, 175.
Goliae Apocalypsis, quoted, 98.

Gorranus, Nic.,
in Lucam, 102.
Epistolae, 103.
Themata, 171.
Greek Church and Nonjuring Bishops, 111.
Greek MSS., 75, 86, 111, 113, 121, 139, 141,
142, 143, 144, 146, 148, 163, 166, 180.
Gregorius, S.,
Moralia, 12, 13.
in Ezechiel, 34, 101.
Dialogi, 37, 101.
Pastorale, 81, 101.
Homiliae, xl., 101.
Epistolae, 119.
Vita, 124.
Grossetete, Rob.,
in Psalmos, 8.
Dicta, etc., 117.

Hampole, R., on the Psalms, 10 and p. 120.
Haselbury, 109.
Haymo in Esaiam, 20.
Heraldry, 92-95, 193: see Arms.
Herbault, M. de, Despatches, 186.
Hermes de salibus, 182.
Herodoti Historia, 113.
Hieronymus, S.,
in Dan. et xii. proph., 21.
in Dan., 76.
adv. Jovinianum, 80.
de xv. signis, etc., 21. 3, 4.
in xii. proph., 22.
Sermo, 106.
Hill, Wm., 167.
Hippocrates, 127.
Holcot in Sapientiam, 18.
Homer, Iliad i–v, 139.
Horae, 181.
Hörproth, Jac., 92.
House of Lords, Orders for, 168.
Hugo de S. Victore,
Homiliae, etc., 38.
de Archa Noe, 120.
Hugo de Vienna,
in libros Salomon, 17.
in xi. Epp. Pauli, 104.
Hutchinson, 142.
Hymns, 78, 80, 81, 160.

Illustrated MSS.:
Apuleius, 147*.
Bibles, 1, 2*, 3*, 25, 27, 28, 179.
Biblical, 92, 177* (Types and Apoca-
lypse).
Chronicles, 96, 123, 191.
Cicero*, 149.
Clocks*, 172.
Dante, 112.
Funeral of S. Gregory*, 124.
Heraldry*, 92-95.
Horae, 181.
Initials, 9, 12, 107, 118 (S. Francis), 129
(Aristotle), 137 (Vitruvius, Hercules),
157, 178.
Ptolemy*, 140.
Roman History*, 92.
Inscriptions, Greek and Latin, 141.

Januensis, Sermons, 74
Joannicius, Isagoge, 127.
Johannes Chrysostomus, S.,
de reparatione lapsi, 119.
de proditione Judae, 120.
Pseudo-, opus imperfectum, 42.
Johannes Damascenus, S., tracts by, 120.
Johannes Diac., Vita S. Gregorii, 124.
Johannes, Prior of Ford, 109.
Johannes fil. Serapionis, tracts by, 126.
Johannes Viennensis, 182.
Justin Martyr, S., Ep. ad Zen. et Ser., 100.
Juvenal (printed), 138 ; (MS.) 152, 153.

Lambeth, MS. at, p. 104.
Languedoc, Mémoire sur, 183.
Laodiceans, Epistle to, 26.
Lee, Fra., 111.
Leo Baptista Albertus, Works by, 85, 128.
Leo, S., tract by, 38.
Lincoln College, Oxford, MSS. at, 47, 108.
Lollards, tract against, 170.
Lombardus, P., Sententiae, 114.
Lotichius, J. P., poem by, 174.
Lyndewode, W., Provinciale, 98.
Lyra, Tabula in N. de, 108.

Macrobius de Somn. Scip., 90.
Maittaire, M., 92.

Mantuanus, Jo. Bapt., Secunda Parthe-
nice, 151.
Mapheus Vegius, tracts by, 165.
Marshall, Vicar of All SS., Worcester, 18.
Marsius, Paulus, Bembice Peregrine, 156.
Martianus Capella, 90.
Martinus Gemblacensis, Chronicon, 131.
Martinus, Tabula super decreta, 36.
Matthaeus Westmonast., Flores Histori-
arum, 123.
Matthias, Prior of S. Albans, 26.
Maximianus, Elegiae, 150.
Medical tracts, 126, 127.
Melibeus, tale of, 19.
Methodius, Revelation of, 125.
Michael Ephesius, in Eth. Nicom., 122.
Miledunensis, Rob., de sacram., 109.
Miniatures, see Illustrated MSS.
Monte, Greg. di, Letters of, 188.
Monte, Will. de, Works by, 82.
Montfaucon, 144.
More, Sir T., Life of, 167.
Morgan, Phil., Bp, 18.
Musae Admirantes, 174.
Music, 80, 178.

Naldus de Naldis, Bucolica, 157.
Napier of Merchiston, on the Apocalypse,
31.
Natalibus, Petrus de, 99.
Nemi, description of, 128.
New Year's gifts, Roll of, 192.
Nonjuring Bishops, Proposals of, 111.

Odo de Cancia, Sermones, 24. 2.
Oratio Salomonis, 26, 27.
Orosius, 133.
Ovid,
Poems of, 91.
Remed. Amoris, 150.
Heroides, 150.

Palma, Petrus de, 79.
Paschasius Radbertus, 83.
Paul and Seneca, Epistles of, 89, 110, 135,
136.
Paulus Diaconus, 155.
Penitential of Theodore, 189.

Persius,
printed, 138.
MS., 153.
Comm. on, 154.
Petrus Canonicus, Disputatio, 130.
Petrus Cantor, see Cantor.
Petrus Comestor, 3.
Petrus de Palma, 79.
Pharetra Sacramenti, 170.
Philaretus, 127.
Photii Lexicon, 143.
Pictavensis, Petrus, Compend. V. T., 96.
Plautus, Comoediae viii., 87.
Pliny, Nat. Hist., excerpts, 134.
Press-marks, old, 15, 22, 84.
Prophecy, a, 21. 5.
Prophetae xii., Gloss on, 23.
Psalms, Gloss on, 9.
Psalter, Greek, 75.
Psalterium cum Hymnis, 78.
Psalterium triplex, 26.
Ptolemy, Cl., Geography, 140.
Pulleyn, Robert, sermons, 38.
Purgatory, demonstration of, 166.

Rabanus,
in Num., Deut., etc., 16.
in Macc., 16.
Radecliff, Nicolas, 47.
Radulphus Flaviacensis in Levit., 15.
Receipt, 43.
Riga, P. de, Aurora, 169.
Robert of Cricklade, Exc., from Pliny, 134.
Robertus Miledunensis, de sacramentis, 109.
Rome, S. Peter's, ancient drawing of, 124.
Rubeus, Bern., Bp of Belluno, 138.
Rufinus, Hist. Eccl., 109.

Sagundinus, Nic., letter of, 135.
Saints,
English, 78.
Lives of, 99.
of Troyes, 181.
Saxony, tract on, 185.
Scholia,
on Cicero, 90.
on Homer, 139.
on Strabo, 141.

(*Scholia*)
  see Eustathius.
Seneca, L. Ann.,
  tracts by, **89**.
  Tragoediae, **110**.
  Epistolae, **135**; in Italian, **136**.
  Letters to Paul, **89, 110, 135, 136**.
  Epitaph, **135**.
  Verses, **135**.
Sens, use of, **181**.
Sententiae, **114**.
Septuplum, **30**.
Serlo, sermon by, **39**.
Service book, Greek, **180**.
Sharp, John, D.D., **111**.
Sibylline acrostic, **43**.
Slavonic Gospels, **40**.
Sophronius, **144**.
Sortes, **132**.
Spain, Anatomie of, **164**.
Spells, **132, 160**.
Statius, Achilleis, **150**.
Strabo, Geogr. I–X, **141**.
Sybbe, W., Fasciculus morum, **34**.
Synodicon, **144**.

Tatian, Orat. ad Graecos, **100**.
Theodore, Abp, his Penitential, **189**.
Theodulus, Eclogue, **150**.
Theophilus, **127**.
Thomas Aquinas, S., works by, **35, 36**.
  excerpts, **47**.
  Summa I, **116**.
  super Dionysium, **131**.

Tirollus, Jo., Antiquitates, **92**.
  de ortu et heroum, **93–95**.
Trinity, arms of the, **117**.
Troyes, Saints of, **181**.
Types, illustrations of, **177**.

Vegetius de re militari, **131**.
Venetian nobles, names of, **137, 156, 193**.
Vienna, H. de, *see* Hugo.
Vincent of Beauvais, de consol. mortis, etc.,
  119.
Vitae Sanctorum, **99**.
Vitruvius, **137**.

Wallensis super Psalmos, **32**.
Walpole, H., tract by, **184**.
Waurin, Ph. de, History, **187**.
Whethamstede, Abbot, **103**.
Willelmus de Monte,
  liber numeralis, **82**.
  de similitudinibus, **82**.
Wisbech, **34**.
Wodeford, John, tracts by, **47**.
Wodehouse, **24**.
Worcester, **18**.
Worth, Will., **100**.
Wotton, Sir H., Letters of, **188**.
Wuluric, S., Life of, **109**.
Wyatt's conspiracy, poem on, **148**.
Wycliff, Jo., **47**.

Xenophon, Cyrop. and Anab., **142**.

CAMBRIDGE: PRINTED BY J. AND C. F. CLAY, AT THE UNIVERSITY PRESS.